At Issue

Why Is Autism on the Rise?

Other Books in the At Issue Series:

At Issue

Why Is Autism on the Rise?

Clay Farris Naff, Book Editor

GREENHAVEN PRESS
A part of Gale, Cengage Learning

GALE
CENGAGE Learning·

Farmington Hills, Mich • San Francisco • New York • Waterville, Maine
Meriden, Conn • Mason, Ohio • Chicago

Elizabeth Des Chenes, *Director, Content Strategy*
Cynthia Sanner, *Publisher*
Douglas Dentino, *Manager, New Product*

LIBRARY OF CONGRESS CATALOGING-IN-PUBLICATION DATA

Why is autism on the rise? / Clay Farris Naff, book editor.
      pages cm. -- (At issue)
   Includes bibliographical references and index.
   ISBN 978-0-7377-6870-1 (hardcover) -- ISBN 978-0-7377-6871-8 (pbk.)
   1. Autism. 2. Autism--Etiology. 3. Autism in children--Etiology. I. Naff, Clay Farris, editor of compilation.
   RC553.A88W4585 2014
   616.85'882--dc23

2013044289

Printed in the United States of America
1 2 3 4 5 6 7 18 17 16 15 14

Contents

Introduction

Autism is among the most mysterious and heart-rending of developmental disorders. All parents want their child to be perfect, and all parents have to accept that, like themselves, their kids are merely human. Yet autism tests parental love like no other condition.

"We felt so angry that we had this beautiful child who was so loving and giving but who was locked in his own mind."

So says a mother of her four-year-old autistic son, Lochlan, in an interview published by the Nemours Foundation. Paige and her husband, Iain, have enrolled their son in special education classes and have begun taking a weekly class that helps them understand how to best help him. It's helped them, too, but it doesn't take away the pain of autism in their lives.

"When we find ourselves getting frustrated and angry, we think about how Loch feels: what's it like for him? That's when Iain and I realize that we can't fall apart, we can't let him down, and we have to be strong and do what's best for him."[1]

It is likely that autism has afflicted children throughout history, yet the condition has only had a name since 1944. No sooner was it identified then it morphed into a whole range of linked syndromes, known as the Autism Spectrum Disorder (ASD). Even as this book goes to press, the American Psychiatric Association is set to reclassify some of the disorders that appear on the spectrum in its official manual of diagnosis, known as DSM-5.

As things stand, a diagnosis of autism may apply to a young man like "Trent," who has never spoken, never returned a hug, never paid the least attention to a fellow human being and yet who erupts in fearful howls at something as seemingly trivial as a flashing light, and who sometimes begins to hit himself in the face for no apparent reason. Or it may mean a young man like "Lou," who seems shy and awkward around other people, rarely making eye contact, yet who is able to have a conversation in a dull, monotonal voice. For all his social limitations, however, "Lou" is an acknowledged genius at music. His mastery of several instruments is far beyond his years, and he spends hours in skillful improvisation.

These examples are meant to offer a contrast but not to define endpoints on the so-called spectrum. Indeed, it is unfortunate that such a linear term has been applied to a phenomenon that encompasses so much variety in people diagnosed with the disorder.

Yet, terminology is the least of disagreements swirling around autism. While the medical establishment roils over which syndromes to include and which to exclude in the spectrum, researchers and medical providers battle over causes and treatments. As this volume shows, autism has given rise to a cornucopia of theories ranging from the dangerously crackpot to the evidently promising.

Whatever their view, people are passionate about the stand they take on autism. One reason is that it appears to be on the rise. The prevalence of diagnosed cases in the United States has jumped from one in one hundred and fifty children in 2002 to one in eighty-eight children in 2012. Less than a year later, in March 2013, the federal Centers for Disease Control and Prevention (CDC) concluded from a survey of parents that the prevalence may be as high as one in fifty children. Understandably, this leads to talk of an epidemic, widespread parental fears, and angry public hearings on finding the cause and coming up with a cure for autism and its related conditions.

However, as with so much else with the mysterious syndrome of autism, it's not even clear that there is a rising incidence. While some argue passionately that environmental pollutants are driving the number of cases up, others are deeply skeptical of such claims. Biologist and writer Emily Willingham speaks dismissively of "our nation's growing chemophobia." Rather than put the blame on the boogeyman of toxins, she and others argue that the rise in autism is actually a rise in diagnoses. After all, they note, the very first discernment of autism came less than a century ago, but the condition has likely been present in humanity throughout history. Moreover, in less compassionate times autistic children stood less chance of surviving into adulthood. It's no surprise, then, that more cases are being discovered now.

Others, however, insist that the undeniable rise in chemical pollutants in our environment is to blame. Some focus on vaccines as the culprit, though numerous large-scale studies have failed to find any link between vaccination and autism.

Amid the din and fury of debate, some authentically hopeful notes can be heard. Science, which in essence consists of the reduction of error though the methodical investigation of evidence, has honed in on evidence that specific brain malfunctions may give rise to autism and that may be receptive to some treatments.

V.S. Ramachandran, director of the Center for Brain and Cognition at the University of California-San Diego, has advanced a hypothesis that malfunctioning mirror neurons may be the root cause of autism. Mirror neurons are a special class of brain cells that fire in response to the observed actions of others. They produce, for example, the vicarious thrill of watching an NBA star slam-dunk a basketball without the viewer ever leaving the couch.

Mirror neurons are responsible for a wide range of distinctively human behaviors and feelings that all cluster around an understanding of what it's like to be someone else—the so-called theory of mind. Among these are empathy, language-learning, mimicry, and anticipating another person's actions.

Ramachandran and his colleagues noticed that the symptoms of autism align closely with deficits in these abilities. They carried out brain-monitoring studies and found that, indeed, mirror neurons in autistic children appear to be malfunctioning. But there is more to it than that. They also found evidence that the brains of autistic children do not process emotions normally, so that some trivial events, such as a flashing light, can trigger a cascade of emotions resulting in panic, or conversely that some attention-grabbing images, such as the eyes of other people, fail to trigger any emotional response at all and are ignored.

These findings have yet to be validated by other research, as Ramachandran himself acknowledges. "Clearly, we need more experiments to resolve these issues," he writes. However, he goes on to say, "Whatever the underlying mechanisms turn out to be, our results strongly suggest that children with autism have a dysfunctional mirror-neuron system that may help explain many features of the syndrome."[2]

Even if this view becomes widely accepted, it doesn't answer the question so many want answered: where does the ultimate cause of autism lie? In heredity? Spontaneous mutation? Environmental pollution? A combination of these causes? We don't yet know with certainty, but these and other important questions are explored in *At Issue: Why Is Autism on the Rise?*

Notes

1. Quoted in "Raising a Child with Autism: Paige and Iain's Story," KidsHealth, September 2013. http://kidshealth.org/parent/positive/talk/autism_story.html#.

2. V.S. Ramachandran, *The Tell-Tale Brain: A Neuroscientist's Quest for What Makes Us Human*. New York: W.W. Norton, 2011, p. 152.

1

Autism: An Overview

Christian Nordqvist

Christian Nordqvist is a medical writer who serves as the chief executive officer of Medical News Today.

Autism is shorthand for a range of complex neurological disorders, properly known as Autism Spectrum Disorder (ASD). They are generally characterized by difficulties in social communication and behavior, ranging from complete lack of speech or attention to others to mild social incapabilities, such as repetitive speech or behavior, tics, and failure to make eye contact. A person who falls on the spectrum begins to exhibit symptoms early in childhood. Some have profound intellectual abilities along with social disabilities. All have feelings and emotional needs slimilar to those of other people.

Autism is known as a complex developmental disability. Experts believe that autism presents itself during the first three years of a person's life. The condition is the result of a neurological disorder that has an effect on normal brain function, affecting development of the person's communication and social interaction skills.

People with autism have issues with non-verbal communication, a wide range of social interactions, and activities that include an element of play and/or banter.

ASD stands for Autism Spectrum Disorder and can sometimes be referred to as Autistic Spectrum Disorder. In this text autism and ASD mean the same. ASDs are any developmental disabilities that have been caused by a brain abnormality. A person with an ASD typically has difficulty with social and communication skills.

A person with ASD will typically also prefer to stick to a set of behaviors and will resist any major (and many minor) changes to daily activities. Several relatives and friends of people with ASDs have commented that if the person knows a change is coming in advance, and has time to prepare for it, the resistance to the change is either gone completely or is much lower.

A Wide Spectrum Disorder

Autism (or ASD) is a wide-spectrum disorder. This means that no two people with autism will have exactly the same symptoms. As well as experiencing varying combinations of symptoms, some people will have mild symptoms while others will have severe ones. Below is a list of the most commonly found characteristics identified among people with an ASD.

The way in which a person with an ASD interacts with another individual is quite different compared to how the rest of the population behaves. If the symptoms are not severe, the person with ASD may seem socially clumsy, sometimes offensive in his/her comments, or out of synch with everyone else. If the symptoms are more severe, the person may seem not to be interested in other people at all.

Having a conversation with a person with autism may feel very much like a one-way trip.

It is common for relatives, friends and people who interact with someone with an ASD to comment that the ASD sufferer makes very little eye contact. However, as health care professionals, teachers and others are improving their ability to detect signs of autism at an earlier age than before, eye contact among people with autism is improving. In many cases, if the symptoms are not severe, the person can be taught that eye contact is important for most people and he/she will remember to look people in the eye.

A person with autism may often miss the cues we give each other when we want to catch somebody's attention. The person with ASD might not know that somebody is trying to talk to them. They may also be very interested in talking to a particular person or group of people but not have the same skills as others to become fully involved. To put it more simply, they lack the necessary playing and talking skills.

A person with autism will find it much harder to understand the feelings of other people. His/her ability to instinctively empathize with others is much weaker than other people's. However, if they are frequently reminded of this, the ability to take other people's feelings into account improves tremendously. In some cases—as a result of frequent practice—empathy does improve, and some of it becomes natural rather than intellectual. Even so, empathy never comes as naturally for a person with autism as it does to others.

Having a conversation with a person with autism may feel very much like a one-way trip. The person with ASD might give the impression that he is talking at people, rather than with or to them. He may love a theme, and talk about it a lot. However, there will be much less exchanging of ideas, thoughts, and feelings than there might be in a conversation with a person who does not have autism.

Almost everybody on this planet prefers to talk about himself/herself more than other people; it is human nature. The person with autism will usually do so even more.

A number of children with an ASD do not like cuddling or being touched like other children do. It is wrong to say that all children with autism are like that. Many will hug a relative—usually the mother, father, grandmother, grandfather, teacher, and or sibling(s)—and enjoy it greatly. Often it is a question of practice and anticipating that physical contact is going to happen. For example, if a child suddenly tickles another child's feet, he will most likely giggle and become excited and happy. If that child were to tickle the feet of a child with autism, without that child anticipating the contact, the result might be completely different.

Wary of Sudden Change

A person with autism usually finds sudden loud noises unpleasant and quite shocking. The same can happen with some smells and sudden changes in the intensity of lighting and ambient temperature. Many believe it is not so much the actual noise, smell or light, but rather the surprise, and not being able to prepare for it—similar to the response to surprising physical contact. If the person with autism knows something is going to happen, he can cope with it much better. Even knowing that something 'might' happen, and being reminded of it, helps a lot.

Some people believe that helping a child with autism learn how to cope better with change is a good thing; however, forcing them to accept change like others do could adversely affect their quality of life.

The higher the severity of the autism, the more affected are a person's speaking skills. Many children with an ASD do not speak at all. People with autism will often repeat words or phrases they hear—an event called echolalia.

The speech of a person with ASD may sound much more formal and woody, compared to other people's speech. Teenagers with Asperger's Syndrome can sometimes sound like young professors. Their intonation may sound flat.

A person with autism likes predictability. Routine is his or her best friend. Going through the motions again and again is very much part of his/her life. To others, these repetitive behaviors may seem like bizarre rites. The repetitive behavior could be a simple hop-skip-jump from one end of the room to the other, repeated again and again for one, five, or ten minutes—or even longer. Another could be drawing the same picture again and again, page after page.

People without autism are much more adaptable to changes in procedure. A child without autism may be quite happy to first have a bath, then brush his teeth, and then put on his pajamas before going to bed—even though he usually brushes his teeth first. For a child with autism this change, bath first and then teeth, could completely put him/her out, and they may become very upset. Some people believe that helping a child with autism learn how to cope better with change is a good thing; however, forcing them to accept change like others do could adversely affect their quality of life.

While a child without autism will develop in many areas at a relatively harmonious rate, this may not be the case for a child with autism. His/her cognitive skills may develop fast, while their social and language skills trail behind. On the other hand, his/her language skills may develop rapidly while motor skills don't. They may not be able to catch a ball as well as the other children, but could have a much larger vocabulary. Nonetheless, the social skills of a person with autism will not develop at the same pace as other people's.

How quickly a child with autism learns things can be unpredictable. They may learn something much faster than other children, such as how to read long words, only to forget them completely later on. They may learn how to do something the hard way before they learn how to do it the easy way.

Feelings and Expression

It is not uncommon for people with autism to have tics. These are usually physical movements that can be jerky. Some tics can be quite complicated and can go on for a very long time. A number of people with autism are able to control when they happen, others are not. People with ASD who do have tics often say that they have to be expressed, otherwise the urge does not stop. For many, going through the tics is enjoyable, and they have a preferred spot where they do them—usually somewhere private and spacious. . . .

A person with autism feels love, happiness, sadness and pain just like everyone else. Just because some of them may not express their feelings in the same way others do, does not mean at all that they do not have feelings. . . .

Not all people with autism have an incredible gift or savantism for numbers or music. However, a sizeable proportion of people with an ASD (Autism Spectrum Disorder) have high IQs and a unique talent for computer science. German software company SAP AG has become aware of this and announced in May 2013 that it planned to employ hundreds of people with autism as software testers, programmers and data quality assurance specialists.

2

The Rise in Autism Requires a National Strategy

Bob Wright

Bob Wright had a distinguished career as a media executive before increasingly focusing his energies on autism advocacy. He served as president and chief executive officer (CEO) of NBC Universal from 1986 to 2001, when he was named chairman and CEO, a position he held until 2007. He established Autism Speaks in 2005 with his wife, Suzanne, after their grandson Christian was diagnosed with the disorder at age two the year before.

The rising incidence of autism has created a national crisis. It requires a federal strategy to address both the individual and societal needs. More research needs to be funded. Diagnosis of children with autism needs to be improved, and access to services, especially behavioral treatments, must be provided more equitably. The needs of adults with autism for education, housing, and an ability to save for their futures must be met. Private organizations are willing to partner with the federal government to meet these challenges.

More than seven years have passed since my wife, Suzanne, and I founded Autism Speaks. During that time, we have seen the prevalence of autism in America nearly double—from 1 in 166 children in 2005 to 1 in 88 today, including 1 of every 54 boys. The prevalence of autism has in-

Bob Wright, Written Testimony Provided for the Committee on Oversight and Government Reform, United States House of Representatives, November 29, 2012.

creased by 1,000 percent over the last 40 years. This year alone, approximately 46,000 children will be diagnosed with an autism spectrum disorder—that's more than pediatric AIDS, juvenile diabetes, and childhood cancer combined. Yet even these alarming statistics may understate the true picture—the most comprehensive study to date, completed last year in South Korea, found a prevalence rate of 1 in every 38 children. The methodology used in this study is now being replicated in South Carolina, with funding from Autism Speaks, and may well yield similar findings. There is no getting around the facts: autism has become an epidemic.

We are asking our elected leaders to recognize that there is a public health crisis racing across this nation and we are not keeping pace. We need a plan and we need it now.

The incremental lifetime cost of caring for a single person with autism is staggering—as much as $2.3 million. The annual cost of autism in the United States is now estimated at $137 billion—a figure that exceeds the gross domestic product of 139 countries. These spiraling costs are borne not just by families but by taxpayers at the federal and state level, as well as by localities. Consider as well the cost to our economy— when one of every 54 boys is diagnosed with autism, 2 percent of the productivity of our nation's male workforce is diminished. The toll on our families, however, is unimaginable. A diagnosis of autism too often leads to divorce, personal bankruptcy or shattered careers. A spouse in Michigan has to give up working in order to care fulltime for a child with autism at home. A family from Alabama is uprooted as they search for jobs in states where treatment for their child with autism will be covered by insurance. Parents in Utah are forced to surrender custody of their children to the state because they cannot care for their needs. And most shamefully, we see the U.S. Marine back home in Texas after being wounded in combat in Iraq having autism treatment denied to his son.

These burdens on families can be addressed, the costs can be reduced, and the quality of life for individuals with autism improved. But it will require new thinking, engaged leadership, and a concerted effort bridging all sectors of our society. . . .

The Need for a National Plan

We are incredibly proud of what Autism Speaks has accomplished. We cannot, however, go it alone. We need a strong federal partner.

Our families are not asking for a blank check from the federal government. We are asking for real help that delivers meaningful results more quickly to our community and with a transparency that provides accountability to taxpayers. We are asking our elected leaders to recognize that there is a public health crisis racing across this nation and we are not keeping pace. We need a plan and we need it now.

I want to say this again: the rate of autism in America is now 1 in 88 children, including 1 in 54 boys. It has become alarmingly apparent that we are no longer dealing with just a public health crisis, but a public services crisis as well. As this population continues to grow, our ability as a society to care for people with autism falls further behind.

Real families struggle every day with autism and those struggles do not end when a child with autism becomes an adult. A recent study found that more than one-third of young adults with autism have no paid job experience or post-secondary education in the first six years after high school. In other words, they most likely live at home with nothing meaningful to do during the day. That is a sobering statistic when you consider that more than half a million children with autism will reach adulthood within the next decade.

But with this sobering reality comes a meaningful opportunity for this country. We know that there are effective therapies that will improve the life-trajectory of people with autism. This means that with more effective translational research and better access to supports and services for the individuals I described, we can help them lead more independent lives and in some cases join the workforce. The trend that contributes to the $137 billion in annual costs can be reversed dramatically for the country as a whole and for the people affected. In the current fiscal crisis, this potential reduction in current and future costs should be appealing to both sides of the aisle and across the ideological spectrum.

Clearly, we have a long way to go in meeting the needs of people with autism and their families. The status quo isn't working. We have to do better, and we have to act now. It is time we commit to a comprehensive national strategy for autism.

Steps Toward a Solution

First, we must continue to fund a robust research effort but should do so more smartly.

We are only beginning to grasp the complex connections between genes and environment in autism. There is now growing evidence that certain environmental factors, including chemicals, toxins, infections during pregnancy, maternal nutrition and parental age, can affect brain development in combination with an underlying genetic predisposition. Recent studies are pointing the way to the development of medicines that could reduce the core symptoms of autism and help improve communication and social skills. Novel behavioral health interventions are being tested that can be started with young infants, as well as implemented later in life to help adolescents and adults develop the skills they need to be successful, productive adults. These new treatments have the potential to significantly impact lives and reduce the burden of autism to families and society. The federal commitment to autism research through the Combating Autism Act (CAA) has been an important first step in better understanding the causes and underlying pathology of autism. . . . What continues to be lacking is a policy that directs funding according to a strategic plan, measures meaningful progress, operates with a sense of urgency, and assures accountability. We need a national commitment—much the way the country has committed to address the AIDS crisis or Alzheimer's disease—to invest the resources needed to solve this growing public health crisis. We must demand results that improve the lives of people with autism today, not just in the future. Through a smarter investment in research we can unlock the door not only to autism, but a variety of brain disorders.

We must develop new and better ways to increase access to early diagnosis for all children no matter what their background is.

Second, we must commit to diagnosing children with autism, regardless of background, no later than 18 months of age, and increasing access to early intervention.

Five years ago, the American Academy of Pediatrics recommended that all children be screened for autism at 18 and 24 months, and that appropriate referrals be made if autism is suspected. This is crucial because we know that early intervention can alter the life trajectory of children with autism. Today the average age of diagnosis remains close to five years. Geography, ethnicity, and race may place a child at a particular disadvantage in getting a timely diagnosis.

Research shows that children from ethnic minority backgrounds must go to the doctor many more times before receiving a diagnosis and thus, they begin receiving services at a much older age. Autism is not something that a child outgrows. We must develop new and better ways to increase access to early diagnosis for all children no matter what their background is.

Third, we have to develop and make available effective medicines and treatments for the debilitating aspects of autism.

Too often, scientific discoveries gather dust on laboratory shelves or are entombed in the pages of academic journals. We need to speed to market products that improve the lives of people with autism. For our part, Autism Speaks recently established a not-for-profit affiliate, *Delivering Scientific Innovation to Autism (DELSIA)*, to help do this work. From Washington, we are looking for the National Center for Advancing Translational Sciences (NCATS), NIH's newest center, to take a key role in fostering collaboration between public and private efforts at real world solutions. . . .

As we develop the technologies of tomorrow, we must fully utilize the treatments and interventions of today. Right now, autism is considered a treatable disorder. But ten years ago, many experts didn't believe it was. Today, we can change the course of a child's development and outcome. Research has shown that early intensive behavioral intervention significantly increases IQ, language abilities, and daily living skills, while reducing the disabling effects of autism and the demands on taxpayers for avoidable costs, such as special education. Autism is not a static disorder; we can treat it and help those affected lead better, more fulfilling lives.

Access to Behavioral Treatment

Fourth, we must recognize and address the disparities in access to proven behavioral health treatments.

We have long known the benefits of behavioral interventions in autism. . . . Yet today families across the country continue to fight for behavioral health benefits, negotiating a complex maze of state and federal laws and insurance company practices.

Consider this—civilian employees of the federal government who for the first time in 2013 will gain coverage for [behavioral therapy] through the Federal Employees Health Benefits Program because administrators finally came to acknowledge the therapy as a valid medical intervention. But over in the military, the administrators . . . offer only benefits limited to active duty personnel. Even wounded warriors who retire because of combat-related injuries cannot get [behavioral] treatment for their children.

With early identification and intensive intervention, some children with autism can lose their diagnosis, but most children with autism become adults with autism.

Here is a classic example of two agencies within the same government heading in opposite directions on the same issue. It is appalling that our military families end up with the short end of the stick. Getting help for any child, let alone the child of a parent who has honorably served our country, should not be so difficult. We can do something right now to help these families. . . .

Fifth and finally, we need to address the needs of adults with autism for continuing education, employment, housing, and community integration.

With early identification and intensive intervention, some children with autism can lose their diagnosis, but most children with autism become adults with autism. To be frank, we do not know very much about the life experiences of adults with autism; only 2% of total autism research funding is spent on lifespan issues. Young adults with autism face real challenges. The majority of adults with autism are unemployed or underemployed, a tragic waste of potential. . . .

Like all Americans, adults with autism should be able to choose where they live, with whom they live, and how they live. But the great demand for housing among people with developmental disabilities and the lack of appropriate support services often force families to decide whether to make their own housing arrangements or wait indefinitely for an adult child with autism to move out of the family home. A broad range of housing and support options must be available to meet the needs of people with autism. These options must not be limited by government-imposed restrictions. Where people choose to live should drive where the government directs our money.

People with autism and their families should have the ability to save and plan for the future. The Achieving a Better Life Experience (ABLE) Act would allow tax-advantaged savings accounts for employment support, housing, and other life needs of people with disabilities. These accounts would be subject to much the same rules as 529 college savings accounts and would not jeopardize eligibility for Medicaid and other means-tested federal programs. . . .

If the list of what must be accomplished seems long, it is because the stakes are very high. On a personal scale, there is this harsh reality: ten years ago, even five years ago, many people in this committee room would have known autism only from what they read in the newspaper or saw on television. Today, they are the parents, grandparents or relatives of affected children. Autism has become ubiquitous. Autism has changed our lives, and it continues to change the lives of millions of Americans. We must face up to the crisis. We are ready to join you as a partner. One in 88 can't wait.

3

Rising Autism Statistics Likely Reflect Improved Diagnostics

Emily Willingham

Emily Willingham is a science writer and biologist. She earned a bachelor's degree from the University of Texas-Austin in English and worked as a writer for several decades before returning to the same university to earn a doctorate in biology. She writes for numerous publications, including Forbes *magazine. Willingham describes herself as a member of the autism community.*

The alleged rise in the incidence of autism has opened floodgates of profiteering, and large sums of money being spent to identify the cause of the so-called epidemic. But the most likely explanation, that changes in diagnoses best explains the apparent rise of the disorder, is largely ignored. Autism and related disorders have a short history in the annals of medicine. Most experts in the field agree that the way certain symptoms are categorized—as well as growing awareness of the term autism—has more to do with the rise of the disorder than anything else. Indeed, the incidence of autism is likely to fall sharply in the near future, simply because the criteria used to classify the disorder will be modified once again.

In March [2012], the US Centers for Disease Control and Prevention (CDC) [released] the newly measured autism prevalences for 8-year-olds in the United States, and headlines roared about a "1 in 88 autism epidemic." The fear-mongering has led some enterprising folk to latch onto our nation's growing chemophobia and link the rise in autism to "toxins" or other alleged insults, and some to sell their research, books, and "cures." On the other hand, some researchers say that what we're really seeing is likely the upshot of more awareness about autism and ever-shifting diagnostic categories and criteria.

Even though autism is now widely discussed in the media and society at large, the public and some experts alike are still stymied be a couple of the big, basic questions about the disorder: What is autism, and how do we identify—and count—it? A close look shows that the unknowns involved in both of these questions suffice to explain the reported autism boom. The disorder hasn't actually become much more common—we've just developed better and more accurate ways of looking for it.

Identifying Autism

Leo Kanner first described autism almost 70 years ago, in 1944. Before that, autism didn't exist as far as clinicians were concerned, and its official prevalence was, therefore, zero. There were, obviously, people with autism, but they were simply considered insane. Kanner himself noted in a 1965 paper that after he identified this entity, "almost overnight, the country seemed to be populated by a multitude of autistic children," a trend that became noticeable in other countries, too, he said.

In 1951, Kanner wrote, the "great question" became whether or not to continue to roll autism into schizophrenia diagnoses, where it had been previously tucked away, or to consider it as a separate entity. But by 1953, one autism expert was warning about the "abuse of the diagnosis of autism" because it "threatens to become a fashion." Sixty years later, plenty of people are still asserting that autism is just a popular diagnosis du jour (along with ADHD), that parents and doctors use to explain plain-old bad behavior.

Asperger's syndrome, a form of autism sometimes known as "little professor syndrome," is in the same we-didn't-see-it-before-and-now-we-do situation. In 1981, noted autism researcher Lorna Wing translated and revivified Hans Asperger's 1944 paper describing this syndrome as separate from Kanner's autistic disorder, although Wing herself argued that the two were part of a borderless continuum. Thus, prior to 1981, Asperger's wasn't a diagnosis, in spite of having been identified almost 40 years earlier. Again, the official prevalence was zero before its adoption by the medical community.

To most experts in autism and autism epidemiology, the biggest factors accounting for the boost in autism prevalence are the shifting definitions and increased awareness about the disorder.

And so, here we are today, with two diagnoses that didn't exist 70 years ago (plus a third, even newer one: PDD-NOS [Pervasive Developmental Disorder-Not Otherwise Specified]) even though the people with the conditions did. The CDC's new data say that in the United States, 1 in 88 eight-year-olds fits the criteria for one of these three, up from 1 in 110 for its 2006 estimate. Is that change the result of an increase in some dastardly environmental "toxin," as some argue? Or is it because of diagnostic changes and reassignments, as happened when autism left the schizophrenia umbrella?

Shifting Terms Are Key

To most experts in autism and autism epidemiology, the biggest factors accounting for the boost in autism prevalence are the shifting definitions and increased awareness about the disorder. Several decades after the introduction of autism as a diagnosis, researchers have reported that professionals are still engaging in "diagnostic substitution": moving people from one diagnostic category, such as "mental retardation" or "language impairment," to the autism category. For instance, in one recent study, researchers at UCLA re-examined a population of 489 children who'd been living in Utah in the 1980s. Their first results, reported in 1990, identified 108 kids in the study population who received a classification of "challenged" (what we consider today to be "intellectually disabled") but who were not diagnosed as autistic. When the investigators went back and applied today's autism diagnostic criteria to the same 108 children, they found that 64 of them would have received an autism diagnosis today, along with their diagnosis of intellectual disability.

Further evidence of this shift comes from developmental neuropsychologist Dorothy Bishop and colleagues, who completed a study involving re-evaluation of adults who'd been identified in childhood as having a developmental language disorder rather than autism. Using two diagnostic tools to evaluate them today, Bishops' group found that a fifth of these adults met the criteria for an autism spectrum diagnosis when they previously had not been recognized as autistic.

Because of greater awareness of autism and the flexibility of the diagnostic tools used, we've recently been diagnosing people with autism who previously would have received other diagnoses or gone unidentified.

Another strong argument against the specter of an emergent autism epidemic is that prevalence of the disorder is notably similar from country to country and between generations. A 2011 UK study of a large adult population found a consistent prevalence of 1% among adults, "similar to that found in (UK) children" and about where the rates are now among US children. In other words, they found as many adults as there were children walking around with autism, suggesting stable rates across generations—at least, when people bother to look at adults. And back in 1996, Lorna Wing (the autism expert who'd translated Asperger's seminal paper) tentatively estimated an autism spectrum disorder prevalence of 0.91% based on studies of children born between 1956 and 1983, close to the 1% that keeps popping up in studies today.

One study in South Korea found a significantly higher rate of autism, but it used a different methodology and different study population. In fact, the part of the Korean study that was most comparable to other studies found an autism rate of .8%—about the same as in other countries.

Toting up these three known reasons for why autism prevalence is rising—consistent clinical prevalence rates across generations, many people who fit the criteria for autism going unidentified, and evidence of diagnostic substitution—we don't need to dig much further to explain what looks superficially like an "autism epidemic" in the U.S. Because of greater awareness of autism and the flexibility of the diagnostic tools used, we've recently been diagnosing people with autism who previously would have received other diagnoses or gone unidentified.

Impending Definitional Changes

And now, after the autism rate's 70-year boom, it may soon take a sharp drop—but that will have nothing to do with environmental factors. The manual currently used to make mental-health diagnoses, the DSM-IV (the "bible of psychiatry"), is in the process of being updated. The proposed DSM-V criteria for diagnosing autism would, according to some studies, shift down the number diagnosed. In fact, Asperger's and PDD-NOS would disappear altogether. If the number of people diagnosed as autistic decreases under the new criteria, as predicted, should it send us scurrying to look for environmental factors that are decreasing to explain the decline? Obviously not.

These evident explanations for rising autism rates don't stop many, many people from hopping on the autism-cause bandwagon to shill research, books, and "cures" for the "epidemic." The MO in nearly every case is, as Baroness [Susan] Greenfield [a noted brain researcher] might say, pointing to a rise in some alleged problem, pointing to the rise in autism, and insinuating a link between the two. But there are two problems with this obsessive focus on misleading connections.

Problem one is that as we now have what is probably a more realistic picture of autism prevalence than ever before, we're ignoring the fact that autistic adults are also walking around in these numbers, as the UK study suggests. Autistic adults may not be seeking a "cure" for autism, which many consider to be a part of who they are, but the autistic adult community could use attention, support, and resources that all too often go to misguided efforts to find one delivish, monolithic cause of the alleged epidemic.

Problem two relates to understanding the causes of autism, another obsession for many people. Homing in on new or recently increasing environmental factors shifts attention from always-present factors that might actually be involved in causing some cases of autism. Does autism have environmental components, such as parental age or interacting factors in the womb? Probably. Do these environmental components have to show an increase to confirm an association with autism? No. Let's not let fright words like "epidemic" and "toxin" distract us from what the data really say. Any true increase in autism prevalence, if there is one, is likely quite small. The data suggest that autistic people have always been here, whether diagnosed or not.

4

Research and Intervention Are Making Headway Against Autism

Alan Guttmacher

Alan Guttmacher is a pediatric physician and the director of the Eunice Kennedy Shriver National Institute of Child Health and Human Development, part of the National Institutes of Health. In this role, he oversees the Institute's research activities in child health and development, among other areas. Among Guttmacher's areas of expertise is the development of new approaches for translating genomics into better ways of diagnosing, treating, and preventing disease.

In response to the rising number of children diagnosed with autism, federal agencies have stepped up their research and intervention efforts. Results over the last decade have proven encouraging. Additionally, progress is being made in research into the causes of autism. The latest studies indicate that an interplay of genetics and environment lead to the disorder. Further research, in public-private partnerships, is needed to complete the task.

ASD [Autism Spectrum Disorder] is a diverse collection of disorders that share common impairments in verbal and nonverbal communication skills and social interactions, as well as restricted, repetitive, and stereotyped patterns of behavior. The degree and specific combination of impairments

Alan Guttmacher, "Testimony before the Committee on Oversight and Government Reform: Autism-Related Issues," United States House of Representatives, November 22, 2012.

can vary from one individual to the next, creating a heteroge-
neous disorder that can range in impact from mild to significantly disabling. Two decades ago, ASD was considered a rare
disorder. Today, with the Centers for Disease Control and
Prevention's (CDC's) March 2012 estimates of 1 in 88 children in the United States being identified with an ASD, this
disorder has become an important national health priority, affecting virtually every community across the country. . . .

---

*[A] simple, low-cost, practical screening tool involving a
checklist that takes only five minutes for a parent to
complete . . . can be used to detect ASD during a child's
one-year well-baby check-up.*

Over the past decade, funding has grown significantly for
research on the underlying biology and risk factors associated
with ASD, as well as research that seeks better treatments, earlier diagnoses and better, more effective services. The NIH
[National Institutes of Health] leads Federal biomedical research efforts on ASD. The NIH invested $169 million in ASD
research in fiscal year (FY) 2011, more than 40 percent above
FY 2008 levels. In FYs 2009–2010, $122 million in funds made
available through the American Recovery and Reinvestment
Act (ARRA) were also invested across these areas, with the
largest proportion of funding devoted to identifying genetic
and environmental risk factors. The first IACC [Interagency
Autism Coordinating Committee] Strategic Plan was completed just as NIH received the significant additional funding
from ARRA, so, with a strategic plan in place to guide priorities, NIH allocated the additional funding between FY 2009
($64 million) and FY 2010 ($58 million) to support a variety
of projects addressing the most critical research needs high-
lighted by the IACC. Including these ARRA funds, the overall
NIH investment in autism research was an unprecedented

$218 million in FY 2010, more than double the funding prior to the Combating Autism Act.

CDC leads surveillance research efforts and establishes United States prevalence for autism. . . .

New Diagnostic Tools

Since the passage of the Combating Autism Act, there has been a groundswell of activity on multiple fronts, from game-changing scientific discoveries reshaping the field of autism research to real-world applications that can help people with ASD and their families now.

One of the main provisions of the Combating Autism Act was support for early diagnosis and intervention. CDC conducts surveillance and reports that the median age of earliest known ASD diagnosis documented in children's records varied by diagnostic subtype (Autism Disorder: 48 months; ASD/PDD: 53 months; Asperger Disorder: 75 months) and varied by sociodemographic group and geographic location. With recent advances, diagnosis by age 14 months is now a realistic possibility, and researchers are actively pushing the detection window to even younger ages. In April 2011, NIH-funded researchers demonstrated that a simple, low-cost, practical screening tool involving a checklist that takes only five minutes for a parent to complete in doctors' offices can be used to detect ASD during a child's one-year well-baby check-up. The checklist includes questions about the child's emotions, eye gaze, communication, gestures, and other behaviors.

More than 100 pediatricians in San Diego County, CA participated in a study using the tool to screen over 10,000 one-year-old children and found that the checklists accurately identified children with ASD and other developmental delays in 75 percent of cases. Impressively, all pediatricians who participated in the study decided to continue using the tool in their practices after the study ended because they recognized the tremendous potential benefit it could provide by identifying autism earlier, allowing them to direct families toward early interventions that can help support positive outcomes earlier in life. Another promising diagnostic tool in development is a simple, 1-minute test that detects eye gaze patterns specific to infants with autism. Researchers at University of California, San Diego who received funding from NIH found that this test, which assesses the infants' preference for looking at videos of moving geometric shapes versus social movement, identified infants as young as 14 months old who had autism with nearly 100 percent specificity based on their preference for staring at moving geometric shapes. These promising diagnostic tools, combined with CDC's health education campaign, "Learn the Signs. Act Early," can improve early identification and provide great potential for reducing the age of diagnosis, thus allowing children and their families to get the services and supports they need when those services and supports can help the most.

Improvements in Treatments

Of course, early diagnosis is only valuable if effective interventions are available. Recently published results from several successful trials of early interventions have validated approaches that are effective in young children, creating real promise of improved health outcomes and quality of life for children with ASD. In a recent NIH-funded study, children from 18–30 months old with autism who participated in an innovative, high intensity developmental behavioral intervention called the Early Start Denver Model (ESDM) showed normalized brain activity and greater improvements in autism symptoms, IQ, language development, and social behaviors, when compared to another group of ASD children that participated in a 2-year community intervention. In another groundbreaking study, a group of investigators jointly funded by HRSA [Health Resources and Services Administration] and NIH reported that an intervention designed to enhance social engagement in toddlers improved social, language, and cognitive outcomes. Early interventionists have noted an encouraging research challenge—the community is taking up new approaches that are being proven effective so quickly that it is difficult to find "control groups" for behavioral intervention trials. While this can complicate efforts to conduct randomized control trials, it is encouraging to know that parents and community practitioners are putting innovative strategies into practice quickly.

We do not know the causes of ASD, but very recent findings comparing identical and fraternal twins suggest the importance of focusing on both environmental and genetics factors.

In addition to early interventions, progress is being made in developing interventions to help adults on the autism spectrum. A recent NIH-funded study showed that a computerized training program for adults with ASD who showed initial impairment in their ability to recognize faces, a disabling aspect of ASD for many on the spectrum, resulted in improved face recognition skills.

Many of these recent advances in early diagnosis and intervention were supported through NIH's Autism Centers of Excellence (ACE) program, which was expanded under the Combating Autism Act. The ACE program was renewed in September 2012, and currently supports nine centers and networks at major research institutions across the country, with two additional ACE awards expected next year. The research conducted within the ACE program covers a variety of topics that are aligned with priorities identified in the IACC's Strategic Plan, including nonverbal ASD, genetic and environmental risk factors, possible links between ASD and other genetic syndromes, potential treatments, and possible reasons why ASD is more common among boys than girls.

Advances in the Search for Causes

We do not know the causes of ASD, but very recent findings comparing identical and fraternal twins suggest the importance of focusing on both environmental and genetics factors. NIH and CDC are continuing to strengthen research investigations into possible environmental risk factors for autism, establishing large research networks with the capability to collect extensive sets of data on environmental exposures and health outcomes, and to conduct powerful analyses to determine which risk factors may contribute to the development of autism.

Population-based studies are the gold standard in epidemiology research. Large sample sizes and rigorous study designs allow researchers to examine many variables at once. Such networks, like NIH's Childhood Autism Risks from Genetics and the Environment (CHARGE) and Early Autism Risk Longitudinal Investigation (EARLI) are utilizing data from medical records, interviews, questionnaires, developmental assessments, and physical exams to explore a host of possible risk factors, focusing heavily on factors in the environment before, during, and after pregnancy. It will take a few more years for these research networks to mature fully, but already, published findings are contributing to the understanding of environmental and genetic factors that may increase the risk for autism. For example, the CHARGE study has identified a number of possible risk factors that may potentially contribute to the development of autism, including: air pollution; mitochondrial dysfunction; immune dysfunction; maternal metabolic conditions such as obesity, diabetes, and hypertension; and maternal influenza infections and fever. In addition to its findings on potential risk factors, CHARGE investigators have reported that use of prenatal vitamins may serve as a protective factor, reducing the risk of having children with autism. In another study, funded by CDC and Kaiser Permanente Northern California, researchers showed that widely-used antidepressant medications taken during pregnancy may also contribute to the risk of having children with autism. Further research on these and other potential risk and protective factors is warranted. . . .

Partnerships Lead to Progress

In all of the autism research and services activities discussed, interagency coordination and public input facilitated by the IACC have played an important role. While I have described in brief some of the autism-related research and services activities undertaken by Federal agencies, it is important to recognize the critically-important role played by private organizations that fund research and provide services to the autism community, and that government, private organizations and the public need to work closely together to succeed in providing the biomedical innovations, evidence-based interventions, services, and supports needed by the autism community.

Research is rapidly moving toward translation into practical tools that can be used in the clinic and community settings to change outcomes for people with ASD.

Examples of joint initiatives that are moving the field forward to enhance researchers' access to data include NIH's National Database for Autism Research (NDAR), which is federating with several other autism data repositories such as the Autism Speaks' Autism Genetic Resource Exchange (AGRE), and the public/private-funded Interactive Autism Network (IAN). In the community, programs like AGRE, IAN, and the Autism Treatment Network (ATN) that involve direct outreach to and collaboration with the patient community are bringing together hundreds of researchers and clinicians with tens of thousands of people nationwide affected by ASD, in the search for new and improved screening tools, enhanced understanding of the biology of ASD and ASD risk factors, effective interventions and services that will help people with ASD reach their fullest potential. . . .

Since the passage of the Combating Autism Act, we can see how the establishment of the IACC has brought a wide variety of research, services, and education expertise to a challenging area and has served to focus efforts across the Federal government, also fostering collaboration with private efforts. This remarkable effort continues to bring Federal agency representatives, parents, people with ASD, clinicians, scientists, and others together to work as an interactive team to address this critical issue. In doing so, it has produced the IACC's Strategic Plan that is updated annually to guide and focus Federal research efforts and catalyze public-private partnerships, while also providing a forum for public discussion and identification of additional needs from the community. With the reauthorization of the Combating Autism Act, the IACC has added new members to participate in the dialogue, in an effort to broaden the outreach of the IACC and infuse it with new perspectives.

On the research front, we have seen some remarkable progress in understanding the prevalence of ASD, developing screening methods and interventions with potential to be used to identify and treat ASD in very young children, and understanding the risk factors that may contribute to the development of ASD. This research is rapidly moving toward translation into practical tools that can be used in the clinic and community settings to change outcomes for people with ASD. In this time span, Federal agencies have also coordinated efforts to enhance critical services programs, identify best practices to support the education, health, and employment needs of people on the spectrum, and develop new mechanisms and strategies to enable broad access to healthcare, services, and supports.

5

Autism—Mitigating a Global Epidemic

Chris Bateman

Chris Bateman is the news editor of the South African Medical Journal. *He also serves as the senior journalist for the* South African Journal of Obstetrics and Gynaecology.

Autism is spiraling upward not only in the United States but all over the world. In South Africa, doctors are reluctant to diagnose it, because they've had little training in the disease. Experts there believe, however, that exposure to a wide range of toxic chemicals in the environment has much to do with the rise. Additionally, some believe that vaccinations and childhood diseases contribute to a disruption in the body's microbiome that leads to autism.

As autism burgeons worldwide, with the latest estimates of 1 in 50 children in the USA between 6 and 17 years old now affected,[1] parents are imploring physicians to go 'all out' for early diagnoses to enable highly effective and timely nutritional and behavioural intervention.

The United States Department of Health estimates that cases of autism have increased 500% over the past five years, bolstering a growing body of opinion that genetically predisposed children are encountering a neurologically toxic environmental 'trigger' that disables them and disconnects them from the world (proposed triggers include heavy metal toxicity, pesticides, viruses, and parasite/viral/bacterial-induced toxicity).

In a paper presented at a recent national autism association conference in the United States, Dr Bryan Jepson (author of *Changing the Course of Autism: A Scientific Approach for Parents and Physicians*),[2] claims that 80,000 chemicals have been introduced into the global environment in the last 20 years, none of which have been tested for neurological toxicity. This timeframe neatly coincides with the duration of the mushrooming global autism epidemic, he adds. Projections are that within a decade the prevalence will be as high as 1 in 22 people. One encouraging sign that increasing awareness of the 'trigger effect' may be starting to make a difference is that children who were first diagnosed in or after 2008 in the USA were more likely to have milder autism spectrum disorder (ASD) than those diagnosed in or before 2007.[1]

According to Ilana Gerschlowitz, the director of the Star Academy of Learning in Johannesburg, which uses applied behaviour analysis (ABA) therapy for children on the autism spectrum (or with a related disorder), her academy gets 10 calls and/or e-mails a week from parents with tentatively or newly diagnosed children. Interestingly, in the Western Cape, 10 children a week are collectively diagnosed with ASD between Red Cross Children's Hospital, Lentegeur and Tygerberg Hospitals. Accurate national autism statistics in South Africa are hard to come by but with just 9 specifically tailored schools in the entire country, an estimated 135,000 autistic children are not getting the specialised education they need. Other better-known facts are that ASD is four times more prevalent in boys than girls and that 1 autistic child needs the same amount of attention as 6 neurotypical children.

Can (and Will) You Diagnose Autism?

According to Dr Dhershnie Gounder, a Durban-based GP (who like Jepson and Gerschlowitz, has a son with autism), most physicians have a low awareness of autism and thus fear and avoid making the diagnosis. 'They've had little exposure at medical school, except as something to exclude when diagnosing. When I graduated in 2004, we had a single, one-hour lecture on developmental disorders. Our paediatric textbook had one line on autism in it. That means for at least those who graduated eight years ago, the awareness just wasn't there. We still get paediatricians who won't make an autism diagnosis because they say the child is 'too young'. Yet every institution involved in autism stresses early intervention: the earlier you intervene, the better your prognosis.'

If you are a child who can't detoxify, any of those chemicals might cause harm. The accumulation of multiple chemicals can act cumulatively or synergistically, one making the other more harmful.

Gounder said one of her 'constant battles' is getting colleagues to stop worrying about 'labelling' a child. 'I'd rather label them than have a developmental delay by losing out of a year or more of learning the essential self-help skills, handling nutrition and treating any gastric-type symptoms so they don't fall too far behind.' A single year for a 3-year-old is a big portion of their lives—she says she'd far prefer to be told her child had a developmental disorder than be 'kept in the dark, hoping it will go away in six months or a year'.

Adds Gerschlowitz, 'There's so much old school out there simplistically labelling it a neurological disorder, calling them retarded, when we know it's a treatable biomedical disorder—there's a medical condition underlying autism which is causing the neurological dysfunction.'[3]

Asked what she'd do if she had a single 'magic wand' wish, Gounder replied, 'Tell Dr Motsoaledi (the national health minister) that every single doctor needs to know what the red flags are for autism, and add a question on autism to the final paediatrics exam.'

Jepson believes autism is too complex to be caused by a single environmental insult, adding that the much-debated removal of thimerosal from vaccines will not cause 'autism to go away completely', because there are autistic children who were never exposed to thimerosal. He uses the analogy of 'the straw that broke the camel's back' to describe how autistic children (genetically vulnerable to start with) are loaded with 'lots of straw' (i.e. increasing environmental toxicity). 'If you're a child who can't detoxify, any of those chemicals might cause harm. The accumulation of multiple chemicals can act cumulatively or synergistically, one making the other more harmful,' he adds.

Biochemical *and* Teaching Interventions Needed

Jepson's approach is to look at the body from a biochemical perspective and attempt to treat the root cause rather than 'just patch a band-aid' on the symptoms. 'We treat the gut. We support their own detoxification system. We remove the toxins from their bodies. We break the inflammatory cycle. We support their immune system. We treat for viruses. We try to heal the tissues. And we teach them.' Jepson said there is a misconception, even among those in the autism community, that one either seeks biomedical treatment or does ABA therapy. 'It's not either/or: you do both. You must remove the barriers medically and simultaneously you have to teach the children (self-help skills). They have to catch up to the stage their peers have achieved naturally.' He firmly believes autism is an environmental illness with a genetic component, and that it's a complex metabolic disease, not merely a developmental disability (a view an 'alarming' number of doctors hold). Autism involves 'multiple body systems interacting with one another' and is eminently treatable.

Gounder feels strongly that many of her colleagues attribute symptoms such as head shaking, lack of appetite and/or attention span and stomach-holding to ASD instead of treating symptomatically, often with dramatic results. She gives the example of a child who won't concentrate or listen and shakes his head from side to side being regarded as 'unteachable'.

'When you look a bit further, you find the child doesn't sleep at night because they have reflux, abnormal bacteria in their gut and constant pain. They won't feed at night. The lack of sleep leads to hyper-activity and head-shaking. When you treat all of that, the behaviour improves and the attention span increases. Often the physician has it backwards, i.e. that the kid has diarrhoea or isn't feeding because of his autism. They also tend not to take a sufficiently detailed history.'

Her own son, Shaurav, now almost 6 years old, was born neurotypical, the only abnormality being that his TB immunisation wound never healed and was still oozing puss at six weeks. Her paediatrician said his immune system was very active because his mother had been constantly exposed in her work, leaving her mollified and 'even excited that his system was so strong'.

With every vaccine administered between six and 14 weeks old, Shaurav's temperature would spike, he'd vomit and have diarrhoea. At 9 months and 1 week he received his measles vaccine. Exactly 7 days later his temperature spiked, continuing in a low-grade fever for 4 and a half days. During this time, he was restless, could not sleep, gagged on food and vomited, became sensitive to textures in his mouth or on his body, lost eye contact and stopped responding to his name. Just before his fever abated, he got a macular rash that lasted a day and then disappeared. His paediatrician diagnosed an ear infection and prescribed paracetamol. Gounder said her son's development 'just faltered from there on, and finally at 16 months I was convinced that there was something wrong. Our paed didn't see it.' She wormed her way onto a paediatric neurologist's very long waiting list and in mid-May 2010 was told that her son 'looked a bit autistic, but it's still too early to tell'.

Today Shaurav uses an iPad to communicate his needs, (e.g 'Mum, may I leave the table?'), attends normal pre-school three days a week (with an aide), completes puzzles, identifies colours and shapes and is compliant; all attributed by his mother to starting ABA therapy at 2 years and 4 months old. Gounder is fascinated by the number of parents of autistic children she encounters who have some kind of auto-immune condition, and believes that this goes some way towards explaining the rapid expansion of autism.

Gerschlowitz described how her son David was born neurotypical with normal development until he regressed at 15 months, leading to a diagnosis of severe autism. He lost eye contact, stopped responding to his name, no longer played appropriately with his toys (repeatedly lining them up), lost his language ability and stopped pointing. 'He became unreachable and seemed unaware of his environment. The first thing doctors did was have his hearing checked, but I mean if you slam a door and the kid startles, he can hear, so we waited in vain.'

She describes how she believes the 'gun was loaded' for David: between nine months and 15 months old he suffered 'countless' ear infections which were treated with antibiotics, he was vaccinated for hepatitis B at five months old and had his two measles shots at nine and 15 months (blood results showed his body couldn't build the antibodies to measles because of weak immune globulins). 'I'm not saying any of these caused the autism, but they helped load the gun,' she explains.

Asked what made the single greatest difference for her son, she responded: 'Treating his gut.' At 20 months David was having up to 10 episodes of diarrhoea per day and was pale-skinned. His paediatrician diagnosed 'toddler's diarrhoea' and promised he would 'grow out of it,' even though several text books list this as a typical symptom of autism. Later she put him on probiotics, and made sure his diet was free of gluten, casein, sugar and soya and that it included specific carbohydrates. To this she added cortisone for inflammation and followed the protocol of several American experts: intravenous immunoglobin and chelation treatment to remove metals.

Her advice to parents is to seek out the best possible expert input, read up on the condition and go for 'one-on-one' teaching, using ABA therapy. Quoting from the book, *Children with Starving Brains: A Medical Treatment Guide for Autism Spectrum Disorder* by Dr Jaquelyn McCandless,[4] she likened children on the autism spectrum to the 'canary in the coalmine cage': 'They send us the message that the environment is too toxic'. So confident was she in the neurotoxic theory that she had another child after David's diagnosis, this time doing everything the experts recommended to avoid toxicity and prevent the 'cascade into autism'. Her child was born normal and continues to thrive.

Notes

1. The Centre for Disease Control's National Center for Health Statistics. Changes in prevalence of parent-reported autism spectrum disorder in school-aged US children: 2007 to 2011–2012. National Health Statistics Report 2013;65. http://www.cdc.gov/nchs/data/nhsr/nhsr065.pdf (accessed 8 April 2013).

2. Jepson B, Johnson J. Changing the Course of Autism: A Scientific Approach for Parents and Physicians. Boulder, Colorado: Sentient Publications, 2007.

3. http://tacanow.org (accessed 8 April 2013).

4. McCandless J. Children with Starving Brains: A Medical Treatment Guide for Autism Spectrum Disorder. North Bergen, New Jersey: Bramble Company, 2009.

6

More Research Is Needed to Assess Toxic Chemicals' Link to Autism

Philip J. Landrigan, Luca Lambertini, and Linda S. Birnbaum

Philip J. Landrigan is a pediatrician and epidemiologist. He serves as the Ethel H. Wise Professor of Preventive Medicine and chair of the Department of Preventive Medicine at the Mount Sinai School of Medicine. He is also the director of the Children's Environmental Health Center and a member of the Institute of Medicine. Luca Lambertini is a molecular biologist and assistant professor of preventive medicine at the Mount Sinai School of Medicine. He received his PhD from the University of Bologna and was a member of the Ramazzini Institute in Bologna, where he launched a new cancer research program. Linda S. Birnbaum is a board-certified toxicologist. She spent three decades as as a federal scientist, two of them serving in the Environment Protection Agency's Office of Research and Development. She is currently director of the National Institute of Environmental Health Sciences. She is also an elected member of the Institute of Medicine.

Autism, along with several other neurological disorders, has attracted a great deal of research into causes but much of it has focused on genetic factors. However, there are growing indications that more attention needs to be paid to the role of toxic chemi-

Philip J. Landrigan, Luca Lambertini, and Linda S. Birnbaum, "Editorial: A Research Strategy to Discover the Environmental Causes of Autism and Neurodevelopmental Disabilities," *Environmental Health Perspectives*, vol. 120, no. 7, July 2012, pp. 258–260. Reproduced by permission.

cals on early fetal development in the womb. Various kinds of studies show that prenatal exposure to various known chemical threats is linked to autism and other disorders in children. Thousands of other synthetic chemicals have yet to be studied for possible effects on neurological health. A workshop, sponsored in part by Autism Speaks, has identified ten chemicals suspected of causing developmental disorders like autism. Many others await examination.

Autism, attention deficit/hyperactivity disorder (ADHD), mental retardation, dyslexia, and other biologically based disorders of brain development affect between 400,000 and 600,000 of the 4 million children born in the United States each year. The Centers for Disease Control and Prevention (CDC) has reported that autism spectrum disorder (ASD) now affects 1.13% (1 of 88) of American children and ADHD affects 14%. Treatment of these disorders is difficult; the disabilities they cause can last lifelong, and they are devastating to families. In addition, these disorders place enormous economic burdens on society.

Although discovery research to identify the potentially preventable causes of neuro-developmental disorders (NDDs) has increased in recent years, more research is urgently needed. This research encompasses both genetic and environmental studies.

Genetic research has received particular investment and attention and has demonstrated that ASD and certain other NDDs have a strong hereditary component. Linkage studies have identified candidate autism susceptibility genes at multiple loci. . . . The candidate genes most strongly implicated in NDD causation encode for proteins involved in synaptic architecture [and] neuro-transmitter synthesis [and various brain functions]. No single anomaly predominates. Instead, autism appears to be a family of diseases with common phenotypes linked to a series of genetic anomalies, each of which is responsible for no more than 2–3% of cases. The total fraction of ASD attributable to genetic inheritance may be about 30–40%.

Exploration of the environmental causes of autism and other NDDs has been catalyzed by growing recognition of the exquisite sensitivity of the developing human brain to toxic chemicals. This susceptibility is greatest during unique "windows of vulnerability" that open only in embryonic and fetal life and have no later counter-part. "Proof of the principle" that early exposures can cause autism comes from studies linking ASD to medications taken in the first trimester of pregnancy—thalidomide, misoprostol, and valproic acid—and to first-trimester rubella infection.

A major unanswered question is whether there are still undiscovered environmental causes of autism or other NDDs among the thousands of chemicals currently in wide use in the United States.

This "proof-of-principle" evidence for environmental causation is supported further by findings from prospective birth cohort epidemiological studies, many of them supported by the National Institute of Environmental Health Sciences (NIEHS). These studies enroll women during pregnancy, measure prenatal exposures in real time as they occur, and then follow children longitudinally with periodic direct examinations to assess growth, development, and the presence of disease. Prospective studies are powerful engines for the discovery of etiologic associations between prenatal exposures and NDDs. They have linked autistic behaviors with prenatal exposures to the organophosphate insecticide chlorpyrifos and also with prenatal exposures to phthalates [softening agents]. . . .

Toxic chemicals likely cause injury to the developing human brain either through direct toxicity or interactions with the genome. An expert committee convened by the U.S. National Academy of Sciences (NAS) estimated that 3% of neuro-behavioral disorders are caused directly by toxic environmental exposures and that another 25% are caused by interactions between environmental factors, defined broadly, and inherited susceptibilities. Epigenetic modification of gene expression by toxic chemicals that results in DNA methylation, histone modification, or changes in activity levels of non-protein-coding RNA (ncRNAs) may be a mechanism of such gene-environment interaction. Epigenetic "marks" have been shown to be able to influence gene expression and alter high-order DNA structure.

Other Chemicals May Be Culprits

A major unanswered question is whether there are still undiscovered environmental causes of autism or other NDDs among the thousands of chemicals currently in wide use in the United States. In the past 50 years, > 80,000 new synthetic chemicals have been developed. The U.S. Environmental Protection Agency has identified 3,000 "high production volume" (HPV) chemicals that are in widest use and thus pose greatest potential for human exposure. These HPV chemicals are used today in millions of consumer products. Children and pregnant women are exposed extensively to them, and CDC surveys detect quantifiable levels of nearly 200 HPV chemicals in the bodies of virtually all Americans, including pregnant women.

The significance of early chemical exposures for children's health is not yet fully understood. A great concern is that a large number of the chemicals in widest use have not undergone even minimal assessment of potential toxicity, and only about 20% have been screened for potential toxicity during early development. Unless studies specifically examine developmental consequences of early exposures to untested chemicals, sub-clinical dysfunction caused by these exposures can go unrecognized for years. One example is the "silent epidemic" of childhood lead poisoning: From the 1940s to the 1980s, millions of American children were exposed to excessive levels of lead from paint and gasoline, resulting in reduced average intelligence by 2–5 IQ points. The late David Rall, former director of NIEHS, once observed that "If thalidomide had caused a 10-point loss of IQ instead of birth defects of the limbs, it would likely still be on the market."

To begin formulation of a systematic strategy for discovery of potentially preventable environmental causes of autism and other NDDs, the Mount Sinai Children's Environmental Health Center, with the support of the NIEHS and Autism Speaks, convened a workshop on "Exploring the Environmental Causes of Autism and Learning Disabilities." This workshop produced a series of papers by leading researchers. It also generated a list of 10 chemicals and mixtures widely distributed in the environment that are already suspected of causing developmental neurotoxicity:

Lead

Methylmercury

Polychlorinated biphenyls

Organophosphate pesticides

Organochlorine pesticides

Endocrine disruptors

Automotive exhaust

Polycyclic aromatic hydrocarbons

Brominated flame retardants

Perfluorinated compounds

This list is not exhaustive and will almost certainly expand in the years ahead as new science emerges. It is intended to focus research in environmental causation of NDDs on a short list of chemicals where concentrated study has high potential to generate actionable findings in the near future. Its ultimate purpose is to catalyze new evidence-based programs for prevention of disease in America's children.

7

Extra Folic Acid During Pregnancy May Curb Autism

Robert Berry, interviewed by **PBS NewsHour**

Robert Berry is a physician who serves as a medical officer in the Division of Birth Defects and Developmental Disorders at the Centers for Disease Control and Prevention (CDC) in Atlanta.

Folic acid, which is one of the B vitamins, is known to be important in preventing certain birth defects. A new study suggests that if a woman takes folic acid during pregnancy, she can reduce the chances of her child developing autism. The study found that folic acid cut the chances of autism by nearly 40 percent. Folic acid is obtained by eating leafy green vegetables, but few women ingest enough to reach safe levels of the vitamin. Experts therefore recommend that women who may become pregnant take folic acid supplements, and that pregnant women continue to take supplements throughout their pregnancy.

Could taking a vitamin supplement before and during pregnancy help reduce the chances of your child being diagnosed with autism later?

According to a new Norwegian study, yes.

Women who took folic acid supplements before and during early pregnancy were about 40 percent less likely to have a baby later diagnosed with autism. The study was published this week in the *Journal of the American Medical Association.*

Researchers tracked more than 85,000 Norwegian children born between 2002 and 2008. Doctors asked pregnant women to fill out a questionnaire about supplement use, both before and during their pregnancies, and followed the children for an average of six years. Autistic disorder was present in 0.10 percent of children whose mothers took folic acid, compared with 0.21 percent in children whose mothers did not take folic acid.

"Autism spectrum disorders are a group of developmental disabilities that are often diagnosed during early childhood," explained Dr. Robert Berry, a medical epidemiologist at the Centers for Disease Control and Prevention's National Center on Birth Defects and Developmental Disabilities. The disorder "can cause significant social, communication and behavioral challenges over a lifetime."

There's been a dramatic increase in the prevalence of autism spectrum disorders, now affecting one in 88 children, according to a CDC report released last year. As the NewsHour's Robert MacNeil reported in his "Autism Now," series, the causes of the disorder are "immensely complex" and not entirely understood. It's generally accepted that autism is caused by abnormalities in the brain's structure or function.

Folic acid, a B vitamin, plays a key role in the first days and weeks of embryonic life, before women even know they're pregnant. Folate, the natural form of folic acid, is found in lentils, spinach, black beans, peanuts, orange juice, romaine lettuce and broccoli. Other products, like bread and cereal, are enriched with folic acid. But most people still don't get enough of the vitamin from food alone.

The vitamin is also critical for reducing the risk of spinal bifida and other neural tube defects. But two-thirds of women are not aware that it's important, according to the March of Dimes—a statistic further complicated by the fact that about a half of all pregnancies are unplanned.

The CDC's Dr. Berry co-authored the accompanying editorial in JAMA. We talked with him about the new research earlier this week.

More Folate, Less Risk

PBS NEWSHOUR: *What did this study find?*

DR. ROBERT BERRY: The researchers found that if the mothers took folic acid supplements before and during early pregnancy, there was a lower risk of autism among the mothers who took supplements. The study focused on a large number of children in Norway over the last 10 years. This compared women who chose to take folic acid to women who did not, for whatever reason.

Is there a way of quantifying how much lower of a risk?

About 40 percent less of a chance to have a baby later diagnosed with autism—39 percent exactly.

What exactly is folic acid, also known as folate?

Folic acid is vitamin B9. It's a water-soluble vitamin that's critical to the function of every single cell in the body. It's an essential nutrient involved in many parts of growth and development, including the creation of DNA.

Only about 25 percent of women are getting [the recommended] 400 mcg of folic acid a day.

The study focused on women taking folic acid four weeks before conception and eight weeks after. Why is that time period important?

We know that folic acid taken during that time period prevents serious birth defects of the brain and spine, because that's when a lot of development of the brain and spine occurs. In the first 28 days after conception, the brain and neural tube structure is formed. So that happens very early, before most women know that they're pregnant. And that's a time when you'd expect other neurodevelopmental processes would benefit from folic acid.

What amount of folic acid were women in this study taking?

The authors didn't say, except to say they were all under 400mcg. I think that means that most of them were about 200 microgram (mcg)—I think that's the usual amount in multi-vitamins in Europe.

What is the right amount of folic acid for women who are trying to become pregnant?

In 1998, the Institute of Medicine made a recommendation that women take 400 mcg of folic acid daily to prepare for pregnancy.

Typical Diet Falls Short

In the U.S., certain foods are fortified with folic acid—grains, bread, flour—is that not enough for the typical woman? Do all women need supplements?

We know the fortification programs provide, on average, about 150 mcg a day. It does not provide the recommended 400 mcg. Only about 25 percent of women are getting that 400 mcg of folic acid a day.

Autism rates have been on the rise for years. Is there a connection to the changes in our diets—eating less fruits and vegetables rich in folic acid—and the rise in the autism rates?

That's not been described as a major risk factor. But there are very few things that are associated with an increased risk of Autism.

Do women with a higher body mass index need more folic acid?

We're looking into that; we don't have an answer yet. That's an important question that we need to work on.

Have there been other studies looking at this link between autism and folic acid in the early days after conception?

Yes, there have been two articles published from a large multi-center clinical trial in California, called CHARGE. They start with autism and then ask questions about vitamin consumption. They found the mother's folate status during that early time period in pregnancy was associated with a reduced risk in autism spectrum disorders. This current study confirms that.

Many readers are aware of the link between folic acid and spinal bifida. Are there other neurological-related disorders that are linked to folic acid in early development?

Yes, there have been a number of papers published on this issue. There's one study on Nepalese children whose mothers were on a randomized trial. They found that those taking folic acid had increased intellectual function when the children were around seven years of age. Another study in India found that at age nine to 10, children with mothers with higher folate levels during pregnancy were associated with better cognitive function scores.

What should women take away from this study?

I think the most important thing is to encourage women to take 400 mcg of folic acid, especially if they're capable of becoming pregnant. This is another example of good that might come from taking folic acid.

In terms of policy, I think that because the recommendation in the United States is already to take 400 mcg of folic acid, it doesn't have any real implications, necessarily, in the United States. It's possible it might encourage women who don't take folic acid supplements to start taking them before they get pregnant.

Elsewhere in the world, it may be taken into account for people considering fortification programs.

8

The Link Between the MMR Vaccine and Autism Is Real

Andrew Wakefield

Andrew Wakefield is a former practicing physician from the United Kingdom who gained global fame as the lead author of a 1998 research article that claimed to have found a link between the MMR vaccine (the initials stand for mumps, measles, and rubella) and autism. The article was published in the prestigious British journal The Lancet. *It created a huge outcry, and nearly half of UK parents subsequently refused MMR vaccination for their children. However, subsequent scientific studies failed to find evidence of the claimed link, and an investigation of Wakefield's research practices found serious ethical lapses. In 2010, the British Medical Council disqualified Wakefield from practicing medicine. As measles makes a comeback in the country, he continues to advocate for his theory.*

Blame for the outbreak of measles in the United Kingdom should rest with the government's decision to stick with MMR vaccines. It would have been better to allow parents to choose vaccines separately rather than in the combined application. Recent decisions in the Italian courts uphold the claim that vaccine causes autism. In any event, the outbreak of measles in the country is not the result of parents being scared off the MMR vaccinations; rather, it is the vaccine itself that is failing to protect children. A public debate would help to clear up the controversy.

The first thing that I want to say is that I did not seek out this latest media maelstrom. It came about because of an outbreak of measles in South Wales in the United Kingdom for which I have been blamed by her Majesty's government. So I did not seek this out but now it seems I have been denied the opportunity to redress the allegations that have been made against me by members of the government; by members of public health and that is clearly unacceptable.

So legitimate debate about the safety of MMR [measles, mumps, rubella] vaccine and the origin of the measles epidemic in Wales have now been effectively blocked by the government insisting that the British media do not give me air time; do not allow me to respond. And that is the purpose of this. So I did not start this current fight.

The important thing to say is that back in 1996–1997 I was made aware of children developing autism, regressive autism, following exposure in many cases to the measles mumps rubella vaccine. Such was my concern about the safety of that vaccine that I went back and reviewed every safety study, every pre-licensing study of the MMR vaccine and other measles containing vaccines before they were put into children and after. And I was appalled with the quality of that science. It really was totally below par and that has been reiterated by other authoritative sources since.

I compiled my observations into a 200 page report which I am seeking to put online once I get permission from my lawyers. And that report was the basis of my impression that the MMR vaccine was inadequately tested for safety certainly compared with the single vaccines and therefore that was the basis of my recommendation in 1998 at the press conference that parents should have the option of the single vaccines.

All I could do as a parent was to say what would I do for my child. That was the only honest answer I could give. My position on that has not changed.

So, what happened subsequently. At that time the single measles vaccine, the single vaccines were available freely on the National Health Service [NHS]. Otherwise, I would not have suggested that option. So parents, if they were legitimately concerned about the safety of MMR could go and get the single vaccines. Six months later the British government unilaterally withdrew the importation licence for the single vaccines therefore depriving parents of having these on the NHS; depriving parents who had legitimate concerns about the safety of MMR from a choice; denying them the opportunity to protect their children in the way that they saw fit.

Were parents concerns about the safety of MMR legitimate? Did they have a reason to be concerned? The answer is unequivocably yes.

And I was astonished by this and I said to Dr Elizabeth Miller of the Health Protection Agency why would you do this, if your principal concern is to protect children from serious infectious disease. Why would you remove an option from parents who are legitimately concerned about the safety of MMR. And her answer was extraordinary. She said to me if we allow parents the option of single vaccines it would destroy our MMR programme. In other words her concern, her principal concern seemed to be for protection of the MMR programme and not for protection of children.

MMR Vaccine Is Dangerous

Now, were parents concerns about the safety of MMR legitimate? Did they have a reason to be concerned? The answer is unequivocably yes.

When the MMR was introduced in the UK in the late 1980s there were three brands that were introduced. Two of those three brands had to be withdrawn hurriedly four years later because they were causing meningitis in children at an unacceptable rate. In other words two thirds of the licensed vaccines in the UK had to be removed from circulation because they were dangerous.

And what is very disturbing about this and this was brought to my attention by a government whistleblower, Dr Alistair Thores, who was working at that time for the Joint Committee On Vaccination And Immunisation, the regulatory body in the UK. He made it clear to the British government that they should not use those dangerous vaccines. He made it clear to the committee prior to the licensing of the MMR in 1987. Why? Because he was brought in from Canada where they were already having problems with this vaccine under the name Trivirix, the identical vaccine to the vaccine which was introduced into the UK under the name Pluserix. And there they had noticed that there were cases of meningitis which were far in excess of those which they had previously seen. This meningitis was being caused by the mumps strain; Urabe AM-9.

And so he advised the Joint Committee not to touch this vaccine: it was dangerous. They ignored his pleas and they went ahead and introduced it anyway. Four years later it had to be hurriedly withdrawn because it was causing precisely the complication that he had warned them of. Moreover, they were asked, David Salisbury specifically, was asked to allocate funds to active surveillance of adverse events. For the government to go out there and to look and ask doctors if they had seen cases of this meningitis. He said no. That was denied and they relied on passive surveillance: in other words the spontaneous reports coming in from doctors and hospitals. That is known to pickup perhaps 1 to 2% of true adverse reactions. In other words it was going to inevitably underestimate the true numbers of this reaction. Hence, the delay of four years for the removal of a vaccine that should never have been licensed in the first place.

It was with that background and with that insight into the practices of the Joint Committee of Vaccination and Immunisation that I took the stand that I did on MMR. I was deeply and justifiably concerned. So the next question is beyond the fact that MMR vaccine is not safe and has not been adequately tested; not just my opinion but the opinion of many; [the question] is does MMR vaccine cause autism?

Now this question has been answered not by me but by the courts, by the vaccine courts in Italy and in the United States of America where it appears that many children over the last 30 years have been awarded millions of dollars for the fact that they have been brain-damaged by MMR vaccine and other vaccines and that brain-damage has led to autism. That is a fact.

If single vaccines were available; if the government had not withdrawn the availability of a vaccine, then there would be no outbreak of measles in Wales.

Now it has been argued by the government that some poor judge has been forced into making this decision that on balance the vaccine caused the autism in the face and in contradiction to the evidence that is available, the scientific evidence. No. That is grossly misleading. Three of these cases at least; Poling, the Italian case, and more recently the Mojabi case, have been conceded by the government experts. In other words the government experts, the government themselves have conceded that the vaccine caused the autism. They didn't fight the case. They conceded it based upon the evidence available to them—all of the evidence—that the MMR vaccine caused the child's autism.

So this isn't some poor judge being forced into a position in the absence of the evidence or in contradiction to the evidence. This is the government's own experts conceding that the MMR vaccine caused the autism, or caused brain damage in this case that led to . . . autism. And what we have are millions of dollars being paid out to these children to fund their autism treatment so when the government says it is not settled cases of autism, please bear in mind that what they're paying for the costs of the autism treatments. The government if it says that is speaking out of both sides of its mouth.

Measles Outbreak Was Preventable

So let me turn now specifically to the measles outbreak in South Wales. The outbreak that the government is alleging is my responsibility, which is clearly in the face of the evidence from Lord Howe in Parliament and for which originally I suggested protection against measles with a single vaccines.

Now it is very important for people to bear in mind that MMR doesn't protect against measles. Measles vaccine protects against measles. The mumps and rubella components are irrelevant. So, if single vaccines were available; if the government had not withdrawn the availability of a vaccine, then there would be no outbreak of measles in Wales, there would be no discussion of measles cases and potential measles deaths. So, the blame for this must lie on the shoulders on those who withdrew the option of the single vaccine from the parents who were legitimately concerned about the safety of the MMR. Not because of me but what had happened because of that vaccine long before I came on the scene.

But there is one problem. There is one contradiction. That is as Lord Howe has said in Parliament, MMR vaccine uptake is at an all-time high. So why are we now seeing measles outbreaks in highly vaccinated populations. It would be very interesting to find out how many of those children in the current outbreak have actually been vaccinated. I suspect many. And this has been seen before.

One of the problems I think we are encountering is that of vaccine failure; primary and secondary vaccine failure. Primary failure—not enough children respond by developing immunity to the vaccine in the first place and secondary vaccine failure—those that do develop immunity that immunity disappears very quickly over time. And this has been seen with mumps vaccine. The mumps vaccine does not work and we are seeing similar outbreaks of measles (mumps) in vaccinated populations. And this is one of the long-term problems of using live viral vaccines over time, taking seed stock virus and repeatedly using it and using it and using it over time that it seems for some reason to lose its potency. And what we're seeing now is what I believe is unintended, unexpected consequence of long-term use of these live viral vaccines; and that is vaccine failure.

And that is something that is really really concerning. It is not theoretical. It has been seen unequivocally with the mumps vaccine. And I believe we are now seeing it with measles. If that is the case then 1) blaming me for the outbreak of this measles case in South Wales is totally inappropriate. It is not addressing the core issue of what you do about live viral vaccine failure, because if the viruses [are] then infecting people at an older age than the outcome may be more serious and there are no therapeutic interventions for protecting those people from measles.

So the government has in effect put all its eggs in one basket and now we're seeing measles come back. That is my belief.

What we face unambiguously is an epidemc of autism; an environmentally driven epidemic of autism now alarmingly affecting one in 31 boys in the United States of America and I saw data from Yale just the other day from South Korea showing that one in 36 children in South Korea are affected by this lifelong severe neurodevelopmental disorder. There is the true epidemic. Do we see attention being paid to that in anything like the same way that the media are applying attention to the measles outbreak in South Wales. No we do not. That is the true epidemic. And that is the one that we really have to deal with as a matter of urgency.

Now what I would like to do, I have been, Dr David Elliman has said that this was my fault and I understand that this morning he went on the news and he was saying that the media were responsible for the latest sort of debate, the latest argument, by giving me some kind of voice. So he is able to make this very very serious allegation against me and then deprive me of the opportunity of responding in the media. That is an extraordinary situation in what is supposedly a free country.

What I'm suggesting is a formal scientific debate in public in front of an audience that is televised. And specifically Dr David Salisbury I would like to debate you because I believe you are at the heart of this matter. I believe the decisions taken by you and by your committee, the Joint Committee on Vaccination and Immunisation, lie at the heart of this matter.

9

Unscientific Claims About Autism Take a Toll

Alex Hannaford

Alex Hannaford has worked as a journalist for more than a dozen years and is a regular contributor to newspapers and magazines in the United Kingdom and other countries. He has written extensively about the death penalty and human interest issues in Texas, where he currently lives. He is a graduate of Southhampton Solent University in Britain.

Andrew Wakefield, the physician who touched off a global scare about the MMR vaccine and autism, has since engaged in a number of activities to promote his views on autism, including starting an autism reality TV show. However, the claims about alternative treatments that Wakefield and his associates promote have no foundation in mainstream science. Claims about autistic children being hurt by vaccines, having sensitive guts and an inability to filter out heavy metals, or responding to hormonal supplements have been tested and found invalid. Not only are these alternative therapies ineffective at treating autism, they can be dangerous and even deadly.

For three days at the end of January [2013], the Renaissance hotel in Washington DC fills up with television executives from around the world. . . . Among the estimated 2,200 people who had paid up to $1,600 this year to try to snag face time with an exec from Freemantle, TLC, Discovery or National

Geographic was an Englishman in his mid-50s wearing jeans, a crisp, white shirt and loafers, and carrying a MacBook. On his badge were the words "Autism Team".

This man's pitch was a reality TV series about autism, and he had a short trailer on his laptop: an autistic child screams; another bites his mother's hand; another repeatedly and violently slams a book against his head. Then a narrator tells us that "every day across the world, medical symptoms of hundreds of thousands of people with autism are being ignored". Cue piano music and the titles, The Autism Team: Changing Lives.

The premise is that the autism symptoms suffered by the children in the promo (Jon, 14, who is "wasting away"; six-year-old twins "still not potty trained"; and 15-year-old Jack, who is "non-verbal and very self-injurious") have left their parents feeling helpless and alone—until, that is, the Autism Team steps in to save the day....

The man in the white shirt and jeans punting the prospective TV series that day was Andrew Wakefield, coauthor of a now notorious 1998 study, published in the *Lancet*, that suggested a possible link between autism, gastrointestinal disease (it was Wakefield who coined the term "autistic enterocolitis", which [gastroenterologist Arthur] Krigsman diagnoses in the Autism Team trailer), and the measles, mumps and rubella (MMR) vaccine. Afterwards, Wakefield called for the suspension of the triple jab, which caused widespread panic and is said by his critics to have resulted in a drop in the number of parents choosing to vaccinate their children. Cases of measles rose from 56 in 1998 to nearly 1,400 in 2008. In 2006, a 13-year-old boy became the first person in more than a decade to die of the disease in Britain.

Guilty of Professional Misconduct

An investigation by journalist Brian Deer found that Wakefield had been paid £435,000 [$665,000] to advise lawyers for parents who believed their children had been harmed by MMR and that he'd given children at his son's birthday party cash in return for blood samples for his research. A subsequent two-and-a-half-year General Medical Council (GMC) hearing concluded in January 2010 that Wakefield was guilty of serious professional misconduct, and that he had acted "dishonestly and irresponsibly" in his research. He had, the panel concluded, subjected 11 children to unwarranted invasive tests such as lumbar punctures and colonoscopies without necessary ethical approval. The *Guardian* reported at the time that the GMC hearings also found that, before the paper was published, Wakefield had filed a patent as the inventor of a vaccine to eliminate measles and treat inflammatory bowel disease. In May 2010, the GMC struck him off [revoked his medical license] and the *Lancet* eventually retracted the 1998 paper.

Since [Wakefield's] notorious Lancet *paper, numerous studies on MMR and autism have failed to find a link.*

In 2001, Wakefield, his wife, Carmel, and their four children packed their bags and moved to Texas, to a house in the hills west of Austin. There he founded Thoughtful House Center for Children to further his work on autism and served as its executive director on a salary of £164,000 [$250,000], before resigning in February 2010 following the GMC ruling. Krigsman also worked at Thoughtful House, as director of the gastroenterology clinic, and left soon after Wakefield.

Wakefield then set up the nonprofit Strategic Autism Initiative to commission studies into the condition, and is currently listed as a director of a company called Medical Interventions for Autism and another called the Autism Media Channel, which produced the TV trailer.

Since that notorious *Lancet* paper, numerous studies on MMR and autism have failed to find a link. One of those studies, which reviewed the medical records of 500 autistic children born in a specific area of London since 1979, found no difference in MMR vaccination rates between children with autism and those of the general population, and no evidence that children vaccinated with MMR at younger ages developed autism any earlier than children vaccinated later.

Another, published in 2008, found "strong evidence against association of autism with . . . MMR exposure". According to the US National Institutes of Health, evidence from the UK against an MMR-autism link has been accepted by the American Medical Association, the American Academy of Pediatrics and the Centers for Disease Control and Prevention.

Claims Based on Shaky Studies

In his book *Callous Disregard*, Wakefield claims his findings of autistic enterocolitis have been "independently confirmed in five different countries". He cites five studies, two of which were authored by his friend, collaborator and Autism Team star Arthur Krigsman. One of those studies appeared in *Autism Insights*, a medical journal on whose board Krigsman sat in 2010. Two other studies were by Italian doctor Federico Balzola. According to the *justthevax* blog, the first of these was a case report of a single adult autistic patient with an inflamed bowel, and the second a "meeting abstract" that "never saw the light of day as a peer-reviewed study". The last one, a study by Dr Lenny Gonzalez, while not reporting finding a distinct "autistic enterocolitis", concludes that "autistic children have a high incidence of gastrointestinal disease".

In May 2010, just a few days after he was struck off by the GMC, I interviewed Wakefield in Chicago for another story. For someone so vilified in his own country, he was remarkably self-assured. He was there to promote his book, which he describes in the prologue as "a story of how the system deals with dissent among its doctors and scientists". Although soft-spoken and polite, he had harsh words for the British medical establishment, which he felt had suppressed his work. In 2011 he issued a statement saying he continued to support independent research "to determine if environmental triggers, including vaccines, are causing autism and other developmental problems".

The fact that science hasn't furnished us with answers as to what exactly causes autism, and that we still don't have a cure . . . [has] created a landscape ripe for people peddling all kinds of therapies, supplements and biomedical interventions.

Then, in January 2011, Brian Deer, writing in the *British Medical Journal* (BMJ), accused Wakefield of outright fraud, saying he had altered the medical histories of his patients to support his claims and that he sought to exploit the MMR scare for financial gain.

Wakefield maintains that the BMJ and Deer are pursuing a vendetta against him, and says these allegations are false. He sued the magazine, its editor Fiona Godlee and Deer in Texas, and although his case was initially struck out on technical grounds, he is appealing and continues to maintain that the scientific research he conducted was not fraudulent.

In January, Wakefield told a media outlet in Austin that there has been a "relentless assault on the few—perhaps five, 10—scientists in the world who are prepared to work on the possible association between vaccines and childhood developmental disorders like autism".

Genetics Versus the Environment

The fact that science hasn't furnished us with answers as to what exactly causes autism, and that we still don't have a cure (although the concept of finding a "cure" for autism is in itself controversial), has meant treating someone on the spectrum has become an area of considerable contention among some doctors and parents, and created a landscape ripe for people peddling all kinds of therapies, supplements and biomedical interventions, many of which are not supported by peer-reviewed scientific studies.

The UK's Wellcome Trust Centre for Human Genetics, a research institute of the University of Oxford, estimates that "genetic factors may contribute about 90% to autism, while environmental factors contribute no more than 10%". Similarly, according to the American Medical Association, "autism is strongly genetically determined".

But some people, Wakefield included, insist that the cause of autism is largely environmental. "You do not have a genetic epidemic", Wakefield told Wisconsin's *Lakeland Times* last year. "The cause is environmental". And this view—that environmental toxins cause autism—directly impacts what treatments proponents of the hypothesis recommend.

The Autism Media Channel website contains videos with titles such as Not Born With It—a reference to the belief that autism is far from genetic, which leads it to advocate biomedical interventions such as nutritional supplements as well as gluten- and casein-free diets (one video is entitled How To Afford A Gluten And Casein Free Diet). Other videos recommend that parents of autistic children cook food using stainless-steel or ceramic pots so metals don't "leach into the food and give more toxic overload to your kid".

In his book *MMR And Autism: What Parents Need To Know*, Michael Fitzpatrick says that a 1996 review of methods of assessment and intervention for young children with autism conducted by the New York State department of health concluded that "special diets, including elimination diets, are not recommended as treatment for autism in young children". The report noted, Fitzpatrick wrote, that there were "no known advantages to special elimination diets for children with autism, and expressed concern that they may cause the child to get inadequate nutrition. . .".

The presenter of many of the Autism Media Channel videos is Polly Tommey, who is also registered with the Texas secretary of state as a co-director of the company, along with Wakefield. Tommey, who recently moved to Austin from the UK with her husband, Jonathan, and their three children, first appeared on the autism radar in 1999. . . .

In 1999, Tommey started The Autism File, a slick magazine and website designed to showcase "anything relevant to autism". One story suggested, "We, as parents and physicians, need to implement strategies to reduce our children's chemical and heavy metal toxicity levels", and advocated the highly controversial procedure known as chelation therapy, whereby heavy metals are removed from the body using "chelating" agents—the presumption being that autism is caused by mercury in vaccines or that people with autism spectrum disorders find it harder to filter "environmental toxins".

Chelation is the introduction of chemicals (and there are several, including dimercaprol, which was used during the second world war as an antidote to the chemical warfare agent Lewisite), either orally or intravenously, which then bind to poisonous metals such as mercury, arsenic and lead so they can be excreted.

There is no scientific evidence suggesting that vitamin supplements can cure autism.

Although it has approval for treating people with heavy metal poisoning, it can be dangerous and is not approved for use in treating autism. In 2005, a British boy, Abubakar Tariq Nadama, died of a heart attack while undergoing chelation in America. Last spring, a doctor in Hertfordshire was given an official warning by a Fitness to Practise Panel after she used chelation on an autistic child without measuring his blood lead concentration or referring him to a toxicology specialist. What's more, an analysis in the US of five chelation studies showed that none provided any certainty that any benefits shown in the children were due to chelation itself, "and not another treatment or just kids getting older". . . .

Promoting Nutritional Remedies

Meanwhile, Jonathan, Tommey's husband, who has a sports science degree and a foundation degree in nutritional therapy, set up the Autism Clinic in Berkshire to offer "specialist autism treatment", including "diagnostic tests" and an array of supplements and vitamins that he prescribes and makes available from his online shop. He also features in some of the programmes on the Autism Media Channel's YouTube page. In one of those films, *Jonathan Tommey—The Biomedical Imbalances In Autism*, he recommends "supplementary intervention" such as "vitamins and herbs" for children with autism. In the same film he discusses chelation therapy. "As nutritionists, we can't use chelating agents. They are prescriptive medications", he says, adding, "They are available on the web. My suggestion is you've got to be very careful doing this without professional guidance, and unfortunately in this country there are not many practitioners that do chelation". But, he adds, "Chelation has been used to a good level of success".

Supplements Can Harm Kids

The Autism Science Foundation, which helps fund autism research, warns against what it regards as non-evidence-based treatments that haven't undergone rigorous, well-designed scientific studies. Gluten-free, casein-free (GFCF) diets, it says, are promoted by those who "claim that children with autism have 'leaky guts' [a theory Wakefield espouses] that allow opioids to escape into the bloodstream and then travel to the brain and cause autistic behaviours". But, according to the foundation, there is no evidence for the claim, "and studies have found that compared to typically developing children, children with autism have no more opioids in their blood.

Furthermore, children on the GFCF diet have been found to have lower bone density than controls, which could lead to osteoporosis". As for vitamins, it says doctors may recommend nutritional supplements to people "with and without autism" as part of a "healthy and balanced diet", but it says, "Use of supplements can be problematic . . . when they are misused in an attempt to cure an individual of autism. There is no scientific evidence suggesting that vitamin supplements can cure autism [and] some supplements (such as vitamin A) can be toxic when taken in high doses for sustained periods". An investigation into alternative therapies for autism by the *Chicago Tribune* in 2009 found many had "little basis in science" and amounted to "uncontrolled experimentation on children". . . .

There is a considerable body of opposition to the approaches advocated in many of the films on Wakefield and Tommey's Autism Media Channel. Steve Silberman, a contributing editor to *Wired* magazine in the US and author of an upcoming book on autism, *NeuroTribes: Thinking Smarter About People Who Think Differently*, doesn't pull his punches. He calls the images of autistic children undergoing violent outbursts at the start of the trailer a "horrifying freak show [which] demeans people on the spectrum of all ages". He believes that Wakefield should be advocating investment in desperately needed lifelong support and services. "The last thing autistic people and their families need is more stigmatising stereotypes—which encourage bullying and despair".

Martine O'Callaghan, who runs the Autismum blog from her home in Wales, is the mother of an autistic son, Cledwyn, who is four and a half. "From the point of view of another mum with an autistic child, I don't like Polly Tommey's idea that autism is something to cure", she says. "The idea that autism is something to be fixed is dehumanising. It deeply offends me".

Kassiane Sibley agrees. She is autistic and describes herself as an activist and advocate for autistic people. She finds Wakefield's concept for a reality TV show appalling. . . .

As a child, Sibley says, she was given vitamin B6 in an attempt to cure her autism. "Take too much and you get neuropathy", she tells me. "That's a fun one, and by fun I mean not fun at all, because you can't feel your toes and your fingers, and they burn, and then you're yelled at for walking on your toes when you're just desperately trying to get the feeling back. If you read anything about alternative medicine, you'll know much of it works on the placebo effect".

Ari Ne'eman, who in 2009 became the first person with an autistic spectrum disorder to sit on the US National Council on Disability (he was appointed by Barack Obama), calls the autism trailer "unquestionably offensive". . . .

As for chelation, hyperbaric oxygen chambers, or even more innocuous treatments such as dietary supplements, Fitzpatrick calls them a "colossal waste of parental energy and a distraction. We need to find out what really does cause it, but most importantly what works in terms of helping people with it. That's where we need to concentrate our energies. It's better than chasing phantoms".

10

Autism Is Caused by a Mix of Genetic and Environmental Factors

Thomas Insel

Trained in medicine and psychiatry, Thomas Insel is the director of the National Institute of Mental Health (NIMH), a part of the National Institutes of Health. Prior to his appointment as NIMH director in the fall of 2002, Insel was a professor of psychiatry at Emory University. There, he ran the Center for Behavioral Neuroscience and the Center for Autism Research. He has published over two hundred and fifty scientific articles and four books.

Recent research shows that some forms of autism arise from genetic factors. Various mutations may account for as much as a fifth of all cases on the autism spectrum. Mutations that alter the number of copies of a gene have already been associated with autism. Now, alterations in a single base (or "letter" in the DNA code) appear to promote autism in some individuals. Although no single mutation in any particular gene has been identified as the culprit, it is becoming clear that mutations affecting the development of synapses in the brain are a key to autism. It also appears that such "de novo," or new, mutations can be caused by environmental factors (such as toxins or radiation). The de novo mutations may take place before conception, in the sperm of the father for example. These findings indicate that autism originates in a complex mix of genetic and environmental sources.

Thomas Insel, "The New Genetics of Autism—Why Environment Matters," *NIMH Director's Blog*, April 4, 2012. Reproduced by permission.

Last week's autism news [March 2012] was about prevalence. The CDC reported a 78 percent increase in autism prevalence since 2002. This week's autism news is about genetics—three papers in *Nature* describe new genes associated with autism. For many people, these two stories seem contradictory or, at best, unrelated. Increasing prevalence suggests environmental factors like chemicals and microbes changing over the past decade, whereas genes change over generations. Why is anyone looking for genetic causes when there is such a rapid increase in prevalence? Shouldn't every research dollar be invested in finding the environmental culprit rather than searching for rare gene variants?

The simple answer is that *some* autism is genetic. Autism, like schizophrenia and mood disorders, includes many syndromes. Indeed, we should probably speak of the "autisms." Some of these autisms are single gene disorders, such as Fragile X, tuberous sclerosis, and Rett syndrome. While these rare genetic disorders account for less than 5 percent of children within the autism spectrum, children with any of these disorders are at high risk for autism, roughly a 30-fold higher risk than the general population and higher than any of the other known risk factors. Recent genomics research has discovered that many children diagnosed within the autism spectrum have other genetic mutations that have not yet been designated as named syndromes. Each of these mutations is rare, but in aggregate they may account for 10–20 percent or more of what we have been calling the autisms.

The new papers published today in *Nature* use an approach called whole exome sequencing, mapping every base of DNA across the exome—the 1.5 percent of the genome known to code for protein. The three research groups are members of the Autism Sequencing Consortium (ASC), an international team of autism genetics researchers. All three look for *de novo* or spontaneous mutations, changes in DNA sequence that are not found in either parent. Recent sequencing studies in the general population have demonstrated that each of us diverges genomically from our parents—the process of reproduction introduces variation even beyond the random mixture of the genomes we inherit from mom and dad. People with autism and schizophrenia are far more likely to have large *de novo* copy number variants, sometimes a million bases of DNA that are abnormally duplicated or deleted and not found in either parent.

While individual genes appear to confer limited risk, the aggregate effect of spontaneous coding mutations across the genome is now estimated to increase the risk of autism by 5–20-fold.

The Role of Single Mutations

These new papers go beyond the previous discovery of *de novo* copy number variants to identify de novo single base changes associated with autism. This is tough sailing because there are so many of these changes in all of us and most of these single base changes have no impact. These studies tried to improve the odds of success by focusing on individuals from families with no one else affected (these are called "simplex" families), and sometimes comparing the individual with autism to a sibling without autism. The results are intriguing.

There is no breakthrough or single gene that is a major new cause of autism. But the role of genetics becomes even more evident when these single base changes are considered. For instance, an individual with autism is nearly 6-fold more likely to have a functional variant in genes expressed in the brain. Sanders et al. estimate as many as 14 percent of affected individuals have such a risk variant. This 14 percent is in addition to the 10–20 percent with a large copy number variant or identified genetic syndrome. O'Roak et al. find that 39 percent of these variants are related to a specific biochemical pathway, important for brain signaling. And Neale et al., while cautioning that the net effect of all of these changes still leave much of the risk for autism unexplained, note the roles of a few specific genes as genuine risk factors.

Stepping back from this flood of genomic information, what is most important? First, these reports along with previous publications confirm that genetic risk is both complex and substantial. While individual genes appear to confer limited risk, the aggregate effect of spontaneous coding mutations across the genome is now estimated to increase the risk of autism by 5–20-fold. Complex genetics does not mean modest effects.

Second, the kinds of small and large genetic changes associated with autism are common in everyone. Risk is conferred not by the size of the mutation or the number of mutations (we all have many) but by the location. Increasingly, we see that interference with the genes involved in development of synapses confer risk; a similar change upstream or downstream does not.

The Environment Prompts New Mutations

A third point takes us back to the questions we started with. It is important to understand that *de novo* mutations may represent environmental effects. In other words, environmental factors can cause changes in our DNA that can raise the risk for autism and other disorders. One of these papers reports that spontaneous changes are four times more likely to show up in paternally inherited DNA and are correlated with paternal age. The father's germline, his sperm cells, turn over throughout the lifespan. Presumably, with advancing paternal age, there are a greater number of spontaneous mutations and a greater likelihood that some of these will affect risk genes. Environmental factors and exposures can cause sperm cells to develop mutations that are not found in the father's somatic, or body cell, DNA, but these new, spontaneous mutations can be passed to the next generation, raising the risk for developing autism. In the initial report of the relationship between autism and paternal age, boys with autism were 6-fold more likely to have a father in his 40s vs his 20s. In girls with autism, this difference went up to 17-fold. Paternal age has, of course, increased in the past few decades. This does not explain the increasing prevalence of autism, but it may contribute.

Is autism genetic or environmental? These new studies suggest it can be both. Genetics will not identify the environmental factors, but it may reveal some of the many syndromes within the autism spectrum (as in other neurodevelopmental disorders), it can define risk (as in other medical disorders), and it should yield clues to the biology of autism (revealing potential targets for new treatments). These three new papers on spontaneous mutations are an important milestone in a long journey. In parallel we need to find environmental factors, recognizing that there will be many causes for the autisms and many roads to find them.

Finally, an unavoidable insight from these new papers is that autism even when genetic may be spontaneous and not inherited in the sense that one or both parents carry some reduced form of the syndrome. Perhaps this insight will finally reduce the "blame the parents" legacy perpetuated for too long in the absence of scientific evidence.

11

Robots May Be Helpful in Care of Autistic Children

David Salisbury

David Salisbury is a science writer who heads up the research news division of Vanderbilt University. As a science and technology reporter for The Christian Science Monitor *he covered space missions such as Apollo, Soyuz, Skylab, and the Pioneer and Voyager missions to Jupiter and the outer planets, as well as the 1979 nuclear accident at Three Mile Island. He has received a number of awards for his reporting, including the National Association of Science Writers' Science in Society award. Prior to joining Vanderbilt, he worked at the University of California, Santa Barbara, and Stanford University.*

Children with autism typically have difficulty mastering social skills that come easily to other children. Among these is so-called joint attention, the ability to focus on something that another person is indicating by word or gesture. Researchers at Vanderbilt University have developed a robotic system that can help train autistic children in that skill. It features a two-foot tall robot called NAO, which is backed up by a sophisticated system of cameras and mechanisms that help it respond to the child's actions. The robot speaks and points as it urges a child to "look over there" at a screen or object. Early trials suggest that autistic children respond well to the robot. While human intervention will always remain important, the potential of complementary use of robotics in training children with autism is being explored.

"Aiden, look!" piped NAO, a two-foot tall humanoid robot, as it pointed to a flat-panel display on a far wall. As the cartoon dog Scooby Doo flashed on the screen, Aiden, a young boy with an unruly thatch of straw-colored hair, looked in the direction the robot was pointing.

Aiden, who is three and a half years old, has been diagnosed with autism spectrum disorder (ASD). NAO (pronounced "now") is the diminutive "front man" for an elaborate system of cameras, sensors and computers designed specifically to help children like Aiden learn how to coordinate their attention with other people and objects in their environment. This basic social skill is called joint attention. Typically developing children learn it naturally. Children with autism, however, have difficulty mastering it and that inability can compound into a variety of learning difficulties as they age.

An interdisciplinary team of mechanical engineers and autism experts at Vanderbilt University have developed the system and used it to demonstrate that robotic systems may be powerful tools for enhancing the basic social learning skills of children with ASD. Writing in the March [2013] issue of the *IEEE Transactions on Neural Systems and Rehabilitation Engineering*, the researchers report that children with ASD paid more attention to the robot and followed its instructions almost as well as they did those of a human therapist in standard exercises used to develop joint attention skill.

The finding indicates that robots could play a crucial role in responding to the "public health emergency" that has been created by the rapid growth in the number of children being diagnosed with ASD. Today, one in 88 children (one in 54 boys) are being diagnosed with ASD. That is a 78 percent increase in just four years. The trend has major implications for the nation's healthcare budget because estimates of the lifetime cost of treating ASD patients ranges from four to six times greater than for patients without autism.

"This is the first real world test of whether intelligent adaptive systems can make an impact on autism," said team member Zachary Warren, who directs the Treatment and Research Institute for Autism Spectrum Disorders (TRIAD) at Vanderbilt's Kennedy Center.

You can't just drop a robot down in front of a child and expect it to work. . . . You must develop a sophisticated adaptive structure around the robot.

Inspired by a Visit to India

The initial impetus for the project came from Vanderbilt Professor of Mechanical Engineering and Computer Engineering Nilanjan Sarkar. His original research involved the development of systems to improve the man-machine interface. He did so by outfitting computer/robot users with biosensors and analyzing variations in various readings like blood pressure and skin response to evaluate their emotional state. The information was used to program computers and robots to respond accordingly.

Six years ago, when visiting his cousin in India, Sarkar learned that his cousin's son had been diagnosed with ASD. "After I learned something about autism, it occurred to me that my research could be valuable for treating ASD," he said.

At the time, several experiments had been conducted that suggested young children in general, and young children with ASD in particular, found robots especially appealing. "We knew that this gave us an advantage, but we had to figure out how to leverage it to improve the children's social skills," Sarkar said.

"You can't just drop a robot down in front of a child and expect it to work," added Warren. "You must develop a sophisticated adaptive structure around the robot before it will work."

To develop this structure, which they named ARIA (Adaptive Robot-Mediated Intervention Architecture), Sarkar and Warren assembled a team that consists of Esubalew Bekele, a graduate student in electrical engineering and computer engineering, Uttama Lahiri, a graduate student in mechanical engineering who is currently an assistant professor of electrical engineering at the Indian Institute of Technology in Gandhinagar, Amy Swanson, a project manager at TRIAD, and Julie Crittendon, assistant professor of pediatrics at the Vanderbilt University Medical Center.

The team decided that a robotic system had the greatest potential working with young children. "Research has shown that early intervention, individualized to the learner's needs, is currently the most effective approach for helping children with autism develop the foundational social communication skills they need to become productive adults," Crittendon said.

So the researchers built an "intelligent environment" around NAO, a commercial humanoid robot made in France, whose control architecture was augmented for the purpose. The small robot stands on a table at the front of the room. Flat panel displays are attached to the side walls. The chair where the child sits faces the front of the room and is high enough to put the robot at eye level. The room is equipped with a number of inexpensive web cameras that are aimed at the chair. Their purpose is to track the child's head movements, so the system can determine where he or she is looking. To aid in this effort, children in the study wore a baseball cap decorated with a strip of LED lights that allowed the computer to infer where they are looking.

Robot Directs Child's Attention

NAO has been programmed with a series of verbal prompts, such as "look over here" and "let's do some more," and gestures such as looking and pointing at one of the displays, that imitate the prompts and gestures that human therapists use in joint attention training. The protocol begins with a verbal prompt that asks the child to look at an image or video displayed on one of the screens. If the child doesn't respond, then the therapist provides increasing support by combining a verbal prompt with physical gestures such as turning her head or pointing. When the child looks at the target then the therapist responds with praise, such as telling the child, "good job."

The setup allowed the researchers to test the relative effectiveness of the robot-based system and human therapists in joint attention training with a dozen 2- to 5-year-old children, six with ASD and a control group of six typically developing children. They alternated short human-led and robot-led training sessions and compared how the children performed.

A robot-centered system could provide much of the repeated practice that is essential to learning.

The test found that the children in both groups spent more time looking at the robot than they spent looking at the human therapist. During the human-led sessions, the children in the control group spent significantly more time watching the therapist than the children with ASD did. In the robot-led sessions, however, both groups spent about the same amount of time looking at the robot.

"The children's engagement with the robot was excellent," Crittendon said, "and we saw improvements across the board in both groups."

Able to Adapt to Child's Responses

One of the key elements of ARIA is its closed loop design. The robot adapts its behavior to each child automatically depending on how he or she is responding. "There is a saying in the field, 'If you've seen one child with ASD, you've seen one child with ASD.' So one size does not fit all. To be useful, the system must be adaptive," Warren said.

The cost of robotic systems like this will continue to come down in the future so it should easily pay for itself by supplementing human intervention. In addition, ARIA is not designed to replace human therapists, who are in short supply, but to leverage their efforts. "A therapist does many things that robots can't do," said Sarkar. "But a robot-centered system could provide much of the repeated practice that is essential to learning. The cost of robotic systems like this will continue to come down in the future so it should easily pay for itself by supplementing human intervention."

Warren hopes that robotic systems can act as an "accelerant technology" that actually increases the rate at which children with ASD learn the social skills that they need. Encouraged by the success of this current study, Sarkar and Warren have started developing robot-mediated autism intervention systems that will address other deficits of children with autism such as imitation learning, role playing and sharing.

The research was supported by a Vanderbilt University Innovation and Discovery in Engineering and Science (IDEAS) grant, National Science Foundation award 0967170, National Institutes of Health award 1R01MH091102-01A1 and by the Meredith Anne Thomas Foundation.

12

Minority Families with Autistic Children Struggle to Get Services

Martha Matthews

Martha Matthews is directing attorney of the Children's Rights Project at Public Counsel. Previously, from 2005 to 2011, she was a supervising and appellate attorney at Children's Law Center of Los Angeles. From 2000 to 2004, Matthews was a staff attorney at the ACLU of Southern California, where her work focused on civil rights and discrimination issues affecting gay, lesbian, bisexual, and transgender people, especially issues affecting youth. She has also taught at several law schools.

Minority families, mostly Latino and African American, who have autistic children face extra barriers in getting services. For example, a Latino family living in Los Angeles with a six-year-old autistic boy faces numerous challenges for which they are not well prepared. Neither parent speaks English and the family does not have a car. The child has no control over his behavior. He has to wear special diapers and be under constant supervision. The family has faced enormous paperwork burdens and frequent rejections in trying to get services.

Public Counsel has worked with hundreds of low-income, mostly Latino and African American, families in Los Angeles who are parents or caregivers of children with autism and other developmental disabilities.

Martha Matthews, *Ensuring Fair & Equal Access to Regional Center Services for Autism Spectrum Disorders (ASD)*, [California] Senate Select Committee on Autism & Related Disorders, April 30, 2012.

My name is Martha Matthews. I'm the directing attorney of the Children's Rights Project at Public Counsel. [Our] own project has seen firsthand the barriers and inequities that these families face.

The other panel members so far have focused on systemic issues. I just want to tell you a story. I want to tell you about one family whose experience, very sadly, is typical of those of our clients. I'm going to call this young man Angelo. He's six years old. He's a six-year-old boy with autism. He babbles; he cannot speak. He has no control over his bladder or his bowels; he has to wear pull-up diapers. He's too big for the diapers you can buy in the supermarket, so his family has to get special, more expensive diapers from a medical supply store. He can't bathe himself or dress himself. He only eats pureed or liquefied foods. He's severely hyperactive; he can't focus, even on an activity he likes, for more than one minute. He has chronic insomnia. He will sleep only two or three hours a night for weeks at a time. He cannot play or interact socially with others. He needs close supervision due to tantrums, self-harming behaviors, and a tendency to wander away from the adults who are supervising him.

They sent the family a two-page, single-spaced letter in English, which I as a lawyer had trouble understanding, explaining the denial and offering the family weekly group classes and behavior management.

Enormous Difficulties

Those of us here who are parents, imagine the challenges of taking care of this child. Even with the education we have, the connections, the resources, family support, everything we've got, imagine what it would be like to have this child.

Now imagine what it's like for Angelo's actual parents. His father is a laborer; his mother is a seamstress. They both are monolingual in Spanish. They live in a low-income area in Los Angeles and they do not have a car. When this family came to Public Counsel for help, Angelo was six years old. He was receiving neither special education nor regional center services, despite his obvious eligibility for both. We got them a pro bono attorney. He started receiving special education services. That part was taken care of. For six months, the skilled advocates that I supervise tried to get services for this family from regional center.

This is their experience: The family asked for in-home behavior intervention services. These are services where someone, a trained person, comes into your home and helps you learn to deal with these challenging behaviors. The regional center said, well, the insomnia and the feeding problems, those are medical, not developmental. Go away. Go to a doctor. All right. Get services for that.

So they went; they went to a doctor. The doctors tried medications. They got two letters from doctors saying, no, these problems are developmental, not medical in origin. There's nothing we as physicians can do about it. So they went back to regional center. Regional center still refused to provide in-home behavior interventions. Instead, they sent the family a two-page, single-spaced letter in English, which I as a lawyer had trouble understanding, explaining the denial, and offering the family weekly group classes in behavior management, saying that they had to attend these classes, which are generic—they're not individualized for that child—try the techniques taught in the classes. And then if that failed, come back again to seek in-home services. Now remember, the parents are just barely making it as a laborer and a seamstress. They're required to attend ten group classes that are not— they're scheduled completely without regard to their work and other obligations.

No Diapers, No Bus Pass

Okay. Next experience. As I said, Angelo requires diapers, which are expensive, because they're diapers for a six year old. Regional center said, well, Medi-Cal should pay. Go to your Medi-Cal HMO. Well, their Medi-Cal HMO did not offer reimbursement for diapers so the family had to switch their healthcare provider from the HMO to fee for service. Well, to do that, they had to get a medical exemption form signed by their doctor so they did that. So then, once with the new fee-for-service Medi-Cal, they then had to find a provider that would be willing to submit a funding request to Medi-Cal to get the diapers covered. All of this took three months. Regional center refused to provide any funding for the diapers in the interim, all right?

Angelo's family ended up with far less from regional center than a white middle-class child with the same disability would have received a few miles away in a more affluent part of Los Angeles. This is wrong.

When the family asked for help with transportation, because Angelo had all kinds of doctors and treatment and therapy appointments—the family doesn't have a car—regional center said, no, we're not giving you a bus pass. Go apply for City Ride. City Ride said, okay. Can you give us some written documentation of your child's disability? They go back to regional center. Can you give us a letter saying that Angelo is disabled and we need this transportation? No, we're not going to give you any documentation. Go to the Social Security Administration and get a letter certifying this child's disability.

So I'm proud of my attorneys. I'm proud of my project. We worked with this family for six months. What did we get?

One month of diapers, one month of bus passes, and ten group behavior management classes, even with our help. That's all they got.

This story illustrates the Catch 22s, the runarounds, the denials that less privileged families experience in seeking regional center services. And if you don't believe that all of this happened to one real family, I brought the original documentation with me.

Unlike the more affluent family featured in the LA *Times*, Angelo's parents could not quit their jobs, search the internet, network with other parents, basically make it their fulltime occupation to get regional center services for their child. And yet, if you look at the LA *Times* article, the quotes from regional center directors, oh, *those* families, those minorities families. They only take minimal advantage of the services available. They can't come to terms with their child's diagnosis. Okay. So we're blaming the families for being in denial. Those families, they can't participate as required in orientations or therapy sessions. Again, the response from regional center officials really struck me as particularly insensitive, given our real experiences with these families, right? It is not their fault that they are put through this kind of runaround.

An Unequal Deal

Even with our help, Angelo's family ended up with far less from regional center than a white middle-class child with the same disability would have received a few miles away in a more affluent part of Los Angeles. This is wrong. We and the Special Needs Network have submitted joint recommendations to change this tragic inequity in which children and families who are already disadvantaged by race and poverty get the least from the regional center service system, and more privileged—I mean, it's exactly the opposite of what it should be.

Organizations to Contact

The editors have compiled the following list of organizations concerned with the issues debated in this book. The descriptions are derived from materials provided by the organizations. All have publications or information available for interested readers. The list was compiled on the date of publication of the present volume; names, addresses, phone and fax numbers, and e-mail and Internet addresses may change. Be aware that many organizations take several weeks or longer to respond to inquiries, so allow as much time as possible.

Autism Research Institute (ARI)
4182 Adams Ave., San Diego, CA   92116
(619) 281-7165
e-mail: info@autism.com
website: www.autism.com

Founded in California by Bernard Rimland, Autism Research Institute (ARI) is dedicated to conducting research and to disseminating the results of research on the causes of autism and on methods of preventing, diagnosing, and treating autism and other severe behavioral disorders. It also provides information to parents and professionals throughout the world, including articles, news, videos, and more, much of which is available on its website.

The Autism Society
4340 East-West Hwy., Suite 350, Bethesda, MD   20814
(800) 328-8476
website: www.autism-society.org

The Autism Society was founded in 1965 by parents of children with autism. It has since grown to become the nation's leading grassroots autism organization. It aims to improve the lives of all those affected by autism. It does so by through advocacy, public education, and national conferences.

Autism Speaks

1 East 33rd St., 4th Floor, New York, NY   10016
(212) 252-8584 • fax: (212) 252-8676
e-mail: editors@autismspeaks.org
website: www.autismspeaks.org

Autism Speaks is dedicated to funding global biomedical research into the causes, prevention, treatments, and a possible cure for autism. It strives to raise public awareness about autism and its effects on individuals, families, and society. It was founded in 2005 by television executive Bob Wright and his wife, Suzanne, who are grandparents of a child with autism.

Center for Autism and Related Disorders (CARD)

19019 Ventura Blvd., Suite 300, Tarzana, CA   91356
(818) 345-2345 • fax: (818) 758-8015
website: www.centerforautism.com

Center for Autism and Related Disorders (CARD) is among the world's largest and most experienced organizations effectively treating children with autism and related disorders. It makes use of Applied Behavior Analysis (ABA), a process of systematically applying interventions based on the principles of learning theory to improve socially significant behaviors of autistic children. Following ABA treatment, CARD develops individualized plans for each patient. With a network of trained supervisors and therapists, CARD can provide services to families throughout the world. Information and research about its services and research findings are available on its website.

Centers for Disease Control and Prevention (CDC)

Prevention and Control, 4770 Buford Hwy. NE
Atlanta, GA   30341-3717
(800) 232-4636 • fax: (770) 488-4760
e-mail: cdcinfo@cdc.gov
website: www.cdc.gov

A division of the federal Department of Health and Human Services, the Centers for Disease Control and Prevention (CDC) carries out research and promotes public understanding of health and quality of life issues. The CDC website has extensive information on autism in a section dedicated to the syndrome. Information is also available in Spanish.

The Help Group
13130 Burbank Blvd., Sherman Oaks, CA   91401
(877) 994-3585
website: www.thehelpgroup.org

Founded in 1975, The Help Group is a nonprofit organization serving children with special needs related to autism, Asperger's disorder, learning disabilities, ADHD, mental retardation, abuse, and emotional problems. The Help Group's nine specialized day schools offer pre-K through high school programs for more than fifteen hundred students. The Help Group's state-of-the-art schools and programs are located on seven campuses in the Los Angeles area. Additionally, its broad range of mental health and therapy services, child abuse, and residential programs extends its reach to more than six thousand children and their families each year.

National Autism Association
20 Alice Agnew Dr., Attleboro Falls, MA   02763-1036
(877) 622-2884
website: http://nationalautismassociation.org

The National Autism Association is a nonprofit advocacy organization run by parents of children with the disorder. Its mission is to respond to the most urgent needs of the autism community, providing help and hope so that all affected can reach their full potential. Its website includes extensive safety information for those caring for a person with autism.

National Institute of Mental Health (NIMH)
Office of Communications, 6001 Executive Blvd.
Room 8184, MSC 9663, Bethesda, MD   20892-9663
(866) 615-6464 • fax: (301) 443-4279
e-mail: nimhinfo@nih.gov
website: www.nimh.nih.gov

The National Institute of Mental Health (NIMH), an agency within the federal National Institutes of Health, provides information concerning mental illness and behavior disorders, including autism and related conditions. The federal agency conducts research on mind, brain, and behavior and offers a variety of publications in English and Spanish. NIMH funds considerable research on autism, and its website has information about ongoing research and many other aspects of autism.

Organization for Autism Research (OAR)
2000 North 14th St., Suite 240, Arlington, VA   22201
(703) 243-9710
website: www.researchautism.org

The Organization for Autism Research (OAR) funds pilot studies and targeted research affecting the autism community. It focuses primarily on studies whose outcomes offer new insights into the behavioral and social development of individuals with autism with an emphasis on communications, education, and vocational challenges. OAR was created in 2001, based on the shared vision and unique life experiences of OAR's seven founders.

US Autism and Asperger Association (USAAA)
12180 S. 300 E. #532, Draper, UT   84020-0532
(801) 816-1234
website: www.usautism.org

The US Autism and Asperger Association (USAAA) provides education, research, support, and solutions through conferences, newsletters, and online resources. Its mission is to enhance the quality of life of individuals and their families touched by autism. Founded in 1994, USAAA began improving the quality of life of individuals and others affected by autism. Since then, it has grown to provide expert guidance and compassionate support, consolidate the overwhelming amount of information families need, and provide networking opportunities for parents, professionals, students, educators, and individuals.

Bibliography

Books

Brita Belli	*The Autism Puzzle Connecting the Dots Between Environmental Toxins and Rising Autism Rates*. New York: Seven Stories Press, 2012.
Uta Frith	*Autism: A Very Short Introduction*. New York: Oxford University Press, 2008.
Sally Ozonoff et al.	*A Parent's Guide to Asperger Syndrome and High-Functioning Autism*. New York: The Guilford Press, 2002.
Stephen Pittman	*Beyond the Autistic Plateau: A Parent's Story and Practical Help with Autism*. London: Lulu, 2012.
Ana María Rodríguez	*Autism and Asperger Syndrome*. Minneapolis: Twenty-First Century Books, 2009.
Alan I. Rosenblatt and Paul S. Carbone	*Autism Spectrum Disorders: What Every Parent Needs to Know*. Elk Grove Village, IL: American Academy of Pediatrics, 2013.
Chloe Silverman	*Understanding Autism: Parents, Doctors, and the History of a Disorder*. Princeton, NJ: Princeton University Press, 2013.
Ken Siri	*Cutting-Edge Therapies for Autism*. New York: Skyhorse Publishing, 2012.

Elizabeth Verdick   *The Survival Guide for Kids with Autism Spectrum Disorders (and Their Parents)*. Minneapolis: Free Spirit Publishing, 2012.

Yuko Yoshida   *Raising Children with Asperger's Syndrome and High-Functioning Autism: Championing the Individual.* Philadelphia: Jessica Kingsley Publishers, 2012.

Periodicals and Internet Sources

Henry Benshoter and Kim Tranell   "Henry's Brother Is Autistic," *Scholastic Choices*, May 2013.

Erin Billups   "Study: Delays in Autism Diagnosis in Latino Children," YNN, October 2, 2013. http://rochester.ynn.com.

Sonia Bolle   "Word Play: Healing Voices," *Los Angeles Times*, April 11, 2010. http://articles.latimes.com.

CTV News   "Mother Who Left Son with Autism Sparks Push for Family Bill of Rights," September 7, 2013. www.ctvnews.ca.

Rodney R. Dietert, Janice M. Dietert, and Jamie C. DeWitt   "Environmental Risk Factors for Autism," *Emerging Health Threats*, April 20, 2011. www.eht-journal.net.

Sarah Glynn   "Autistic Kids May Not Find Pleasure in Voices," *Medical News Today*, June 18, 2013. www.medicalnewstoday.com.

Amy Harmon "Autistic and Seeking a Place in an Adult World," *New York Times*, September 17, 2011. www.nytimes .com.

Virginia Hughes "Genes Associated with Autism Are Surprisingly Large," *Scientific American*, September 23, 2013. www.scientificamerican.com.

Christian Nordqvist "Multiple Vaccines Not Linked to Autism Risk, CDC," *Medical News Today*, March 30, 2013. www .medicalnewstoday.com.

Robert Preidt "Missing Genes May Be Tied to Development of Autism: Study," *HealthDay*, October 3, 2013. www.philly.com.

Mark Roth "Debate Continues: Is Autism Really Growing?" *Pittsburgh Post-Gazette*, October 6, 2013. www.post-gazette .com.

Andrew Seaman "No Link Between Celiac Disease and Autism: Study," Reuters, September 25, 2013. www.reuters.com.

Rebecca Shine and Adrienne Perry "The Relationship Between Parental Stress and Intervention Outcome of Children with Autism," *Journal on Developmental Disabilities*, vol. 16 no. 2, 2010.

Nancy Shute "Desperate for an Autism Cure," *Scientific American*, October 7, 2010. www.scientificamerican.com.

| Fran Smith | "Rewriting a Life Story: Treating Autism Early Can Help Save Later," Edutopia, October 9, 2013. www .edutopia.org. |

| A.H. Solomon and B. Chung | "Understanding Autism: How Family Therapists Can Support Parents of Children with Autism Spectrum Disorders," *Family Process*, June 2012. |

| Dennis Thompson | "More Links Seen Between Autism, ADHD," *US News & World Report*, August 26, 2013. http://health.usnews .com. |

| Moises Velasquez-Manoff | "An Immune Disorder at the Root of Autism," *New York Times*, August 25, 2012. www.nytimes.com. |

| M.S. Wingate et al. | "Prevalence of Autism Spectrum Disorders: Autism and Developmental Disabilities Monitoring Network," *Morbidity and Mortality Weekly Report Surveillance Summaries*, March 30, 2012. |

| Carl Zimmer | "The Brain: The Troublesome Bloom of Autism," *Discover*, March 2012. http://discovermagazine.com. |

Index

A

Achieving a Better Life Experience
(ABLE) Act, 24
Adaptive Robot-Mediated Intervention Architecture (ARIA), 83,
84–85
AIDS crisis, 21
Alzheimer's disease, 21
American Academy of Pediatrics,
21, 68
American Medical Association, 68,
70
American Psychiatric Association,
7
American Recovery and Reinvestment Act (ARRA), 32–33
Applied behaviour analysis (ABA)
therapy, 40
Asperger, Hans, 27
Asperger's syndrome, 14, 27, 29,
33
Attention deficit/hyperactivity disorder (ADHD), 47
Autism
classification of, 7
defined, 11–12, 31–32
feelings and expression, 15–16
folic acid supplementation,
52–56
introduction, 7–10, 9
minority families with, 86–90
MMR vaccine does not cause,
65–74
MMR vaccine may cause,
57–64
nonverbal ASD, 35

nutritional therapy for, 72
overview, 11–16
rates, 8, 25, 32, 47, 76
sudden change wariness,
14–15
wide-spectrum disorder,
12–14
See also Robot care for autistic children
Autism, environmental link
chemicals as culprits, 49–51
connection between, 20
genetics link and, 69–72,
75–79
increased diagnosis, 29
overview, 47–49
research needed, 46–51
from toxic chemicals, 40
Autism, rise in
behavioral treatments for,
22–24
biochemical and teaching interventions, 42–45
cost of, 18
definitional changes, 29–30
federal partnerships and,
37–38
as global epidemic, 39–45
identifying autism, 26–27
improved diagnostics, 25–30,
33–34, 40–42
improved treatments, 34–35
national strategy for, 17–24
overview, 17–19, 39–40
research and intervention,
31–38
steps for solution, 20–22
terminology in, 27–29